Master Photographers

Master Photographers

The World's Great Photographers on their
Art and Technique · Edited by Pat Booth

Clarkson N. Potter, Inc./Publishers NEW YORK
DISTRIBUTED BY CROWN PUBLISHERS, INC.

For Chandra, Jonathan and my son Orlando.

Text copyright © 1983 by Pat Booth

Design copyright © 1983 by Macmillan London Limited

The copyright in the photographs is held in each case by
the respective photographer
The copyright in the portraits of them is held by Pat Booth

Published in the United States of America by Clarkson N. Potter, Inc.,
One Park Avenue, New York, New York 10016

First published in Great Britain in 1983 by
Macmillan London Limited
London and Basingstoke

Manufactured in Hong Kong

Designed by Robert Updegraff

Library of Congress Cataloging in Publication Data
Main entry under title:

Master photographers.

   Includes bibliographies.
   1. Photographers—Interviews.   2. Photography.
I. Title.
TR147.M33 1983   770'.92'2 [B]   83-10903
ISBN 0-517-55011-3 (cloth)
ISBN 0-517-55012-1 (pbk.)

10 9 8 7 6 5 4 3 2 1

First American Edition

Contents

Introduction

Behind great art there often stands a great artist, and in my interviews with the sixteen photographers in this book I have sought to illuminate such qualities, as well as to draw out some of the secrets of creating great pictures. Photography is not an intellectual medium. In the end the work must stand on its own, unexplained, essentially inexplicable. These master photographers have themselves selected and described the photographs reproduced here. This book, therefore, is unique in that it truly represents each artist's essence, showing most clearly his or her perspective, the way that that artist sees his or her own work – which may not, of course, necessarily be the way others see it.

Words and photographs tell much, but in a book about this visual medium an image of the creator can often reveal more. The portraits which I have taken of these masters of their art offer the reader the opportunity to look into the eyes of those whose contribution to that art has been to 'see' in such a different and illuminating way. For me this process of visual and conceptual re-education is these photographers' most valuable gift. Erotic fantasies bring Helmut Newton's images to mind; romantic thoughts conjure up Lartigue's work; brooding landscapes remind one of Brandt; heroic, monumental scenes of nature recall the consummate artistry of Ansel Adams.

In these pages you will not learn how to take a great photograph, but to the dedicated detective the ground will be littered with clues as to how that most elusive of objectives can be attained. First and foremost, all these photographers agree that it is necessary to master the mechanics of what they so often refer to, with false modesty, as the craft rather than the art of photography. Once assimilated, however, it must never be allowed to interfere with the mind's eye, with the creative vision. Nobody can express precisely how the leap is made from a technically competent picture to the kind of photograph reproduced here. If it is true that luck plays some part it is more true that, in the words of Ansel Adams, 'Chance favours the prepared mind.' The prepared mind it may be, but it is also the mind that is prepared to see. When I talked to Kertész he quoted to me what one critic had said of his work: 'Washington Square only looks nice if you happen to be

André Kertész looking down on it.' If these images, words and portraits encourage us to do nothing else but aspire to such vision, and teach us new ways of looking at our world, then we will be set fair on the path towards mastery of photography.

I thank all those people who helped make *Master Photographers* possible. First, of course, there are the photographers themselves. They were as generous with their valuable time and their inspiring photographs as they were in sharing with me their fascinating thoughts, and this despite the photographer's often instinctive mistrust of words and philosophizing. My thanks are also due to my editor at Macmillan, Michael Alcock, for keeping my reins so loose; to my husband, Garth, who was left, literally, holding the baby while I took off around the world; to Barbara Lloyd at the Marlborough Gallery, by whose kind permission the Bill Brandt photographs are reproduced; to Mark Haworth-Booth at the Victoria and Albert Museum; to Barry Taylor of Olympus; to Sue Davis of the Photographers' Gallery; to Helena Srakoćić of the Contrast Gallery; to Di and Arch Cummin; to Robin Bell, my printer; to Tom Blau of Camera Press; and to Yousuf Karsh and Ansel Adams for their kindness and hospitality in Ottawa and Carmel.

PAT BOOTH
Summer 1983

Ansel Adams

Ansel Adams, musician, conservationist and scientist, is the world's most revered living photographer. Born in San Francisco in 1902, he studied the piano with the intention of making his career in music, but at the age of fourteen two momentous events took place which were to change his life: he was taken by his parents to the Yosemite Valley in California, where he fell in love with the Sierra Nevada, and on that same vacation he was given a No. 1 Box Brownie camera. From that moment he became obsessed with the beauty of the American landscape and the need to capture it on film. At seventeen he became custodian of the Sierra Club's LeConte Memorial in Yosemite, the beginning of a lifetime's work dedicated to the preservation of the American wilderness and national parks.

'My last word is that it all depends on what you visualize.'

In 1930 Adams was strongly influenced by a meeting with the photographer Paul Strand, the quality of whose negatives made a deep impression on him. In that same year Adams' photographic book *Taos Pueblo* was published. In spite of the depression it became a great success. Now, at the age of twenty-eight, he decided to give up music and concentrate full-time on photography.

Adams continued to develop his own personal philosophy of photography. A firm believer in discipline, rigorous lack of affectation and the simplicity that can come only from a formidable mastery of all aspects of the medium, he searched out those who shared his ideals. In 1932 the influential Group f/64 was founded, including among its members Edward Weston and Imogen Cunningham. Adams argued that the true task of the photographer was first to conceptualize, then accurately to capture and finally to reproduce as nearly as possible the emotional as well as the objective realities. For this reason he found it impossible to separate the art of photography from its science. At each stage the technique must be mastered, and developing and printing were no less important than choice of subject and exposure.

Drawing on his deep understanding of musical theory, he adapted the language of sound to explain subtle variations of light. From this discovery of the similarities between these physical phenomena he developed in the 1930s his famous Zone System in an attempt to devise a standard procedure for exposure and development that would give consistent negative quality.

Not content merely to produce great photographs, he became a teacher, and expanded his theoretical ideas in a series of textbooks such as *Making a Photograph* and the five-volume *Basic Photo* series (details of these can be found in the Bibliography on page 197). In 1940 he helped to found the photography department at the Museum of Modern Art in New York.

His one-man exhibitions have included shows at the Smithsonian Institution, Washington DC, in 1931; An American Place, New York, in 1936; the San Francisco Museum of Art, in 1939 and 1972; the Museum of Modern Art, New York, in 1944 and 1979; the Art Institute of Chicago, in 1951; the Victoria and Albert Museums, London, in 1974; and the Metropolitan Museum of Art, New York, in 1974.

Today he lives in Carmel, California, where he remains committed to the cause of environmental protection, locked in battle with those who would unleash the forces of pollution on the beloved landscapes that he has immortalized on film. He remains the grand old man of American photography, a genius whose sensitive portraits no less than his photographs of nature establish him as one of the great artists of the twentieth century.

———•———

Could you talk first about the photograph of the Half Dome?

It was taken in 1927, and was the first picture where I felt I had really visualized the scenic effect in my mind's eye. I had only two $8\frac{1}{2} \times 6\frac{1}{2}$-inch glass plates left by the time I reached this location. It was a four-thousand-foot climb with the camera and there were eight feet of snow. I made the first picture with an ordinary yellow K2 filter, which was the standard filter at that time. Then I got to thinking, 'Well now, this is the most monumental thing.' I guess it's one of the most impressive mountain views in the country. And then I said, 'Forget what it looks like. How does it *feel*?' I had one more plate and a strong red filter and this was the result. At first the sky had been rather bland with no depth, no strength in the shadows. Changing the filter was what made the difference.

This question of 'feeling' must be very important to you. Can you expand on it?

Ever since 1927 I have tried to visualize all my pictures before taking them. I think all photographers do that but it takes a long time to be in total command of the technique. There are different ways of 'seeing' a picture. The subject is squeezed into the mind somewhere. Some photographers, however, don't understand the way that the lens 'sees' and the film 'sees'. Eventually you learn how to manage the film, the exposure and the development and how to get the information on to the negative and print. But like any art it takes time.

After your lifetime's depth of experience you must now be in total command of those techniques.

I can always control the picture unless I make a plain, ordinary arithmetical mistake, which happens quite often, or if I forget to figure a lens extension. Or again I may visualize the picture and turn the colour into poorly separated black-and-white values, and so miss the full intensity of the visualization. That doesn't occur too often now, but it happened all the time in the beginning. In those days I didn't have what I call 'image management'. The idea is to control the image on the ground glass – to 'see' things from the point of view of the lens. You just have to 'look' at the world like this or you are lost.

Monolith – The Face of the Half Dome, California, 1927.

The Black Sun, Owens Valley, California, 1939.

The picture known as The Black Sun *is one of your best-known ones. Tell me how you came to take it.*

I was working in the desert east of the Sierra Nevada a little after sunrise. I wanted to photograph right into the sun, planning to use the brilliant flare as part of the composition. I made several exposures with a 5×7 camera and Isopan film; I intended to develop one in Kodak D-23. I knew I might get a little reversal – a phenomenon of excessive exposure – in this negative, and as the sun disc appeared to have slightly less density in the centre of the general flare I decided to develop the next negative in Pyrocatechin, a highly compensating developer. In this negative the disc of the sun was almost fully reversed and has printed very dark. Reversal can be a very exciting effect when it's properly used. I don't think that its physical chemistry is yet completely understood.

Actually 'The Black Sun' is not a good description of this picture any more, because it now means the equivalent of a neutron star, and that's an astronomical phenomenon which had not been discovered at the time I made the picture. But I guess the title will stick!

The picture of moonrise over Hernandez must have been possible only for a moment.

It's an example of a quotation from Pasteur, which roughly translates as 'Chance favours the prepared mind.' I saw this image out of the car window and I practically ditched my station wagon. I had my son and a friend with me and I yelled, 'Get the hell out of the car and help me. I think I have a great picture!' I got my 10 × 8 set up barely in time, as the low sun was skirting a wind-blown cloud bank, but I couldn't find my exposure meter. The only thing I knew was that the moon was 250 candelas per square foot. If I had used a meter I would have secured a better exposure for the foreground and would have based the exposure on that value, but the moon would not have held all the detail it now shows.

I placed the luminance value of the moon on Zone VII. As 250 candelas per square foot was on VII, 60 candelas per square foot fell on Zone V. With Isopan film this indicated a basic exposure of 1/60 of a second at f/8. Adding a 3X yellow filter reduced this to 1/20 of a second. Stopping down to f/32, I gave a 'long' one-second exposure. As I turned the holder round to go for another, the remaining sunlight left white crosses. It was pure luck that I got the first one. I gave the negative water-bath development to preserve maximum density in the foreground.

Moonrise, Hernandez, New Mexico, 1941.

You mentioned your well-known Zone System there. What is it, and how and why did you invent it?

The system is nothing but applied sensitometry, and I didn't invent sensitometry! I worked out a practical codification of sensitometric principles. I was teaching at the time in Los Angeles and I found that it was hard for me to explain to my students what I was trying to get out of photography. Just about that time an engineer by the name of Davenport published a paper in an early issue of *US Camera Magazine* about maintaining consistent negative density of different exposures of the same reflective surface. He claimed that if you first exposed this surface at an average reading of the Weston meter you could consider it 'normal' and give the negative 'normal' development. If you gave twice the exposure and reduced development, the negative density would be the same. If you gave one half the exposure and increased development, the negative density would be 'normal'. It's not quite as simple as I've made it sound, but the basic idea is there.

I thought that if you could express in one coherent scale the relationship of exposure and development you could control subjects of widely varying contrast and discover that you could learn to visualize the desired image.

It's a very useful system. Put it this way – if you have to *think* of every step when you make a picture, you'll be in trouble. It's like music – you first have to get every note and nuance in your head until they become second nature, and then when you play you can concentrate on the whole, on the big shapes, the masses of sound and the phrase and rhythm structure. You are not aware of the individual notes, although you have to know them. It's just the same in photography. Everything must come to you quite automatically.

Can you explain how the system works in practice?

Take those seashells and coral by the window in the room we're in now. I want to record the values, especially in the shadows, as I don't want to lose the impression of light in all areas, and maybe a trace of detail in the bright foliage outside. I can see the picture as a whole, somewhat soft like a pencil sketch, but with expressive values in all parts of the subject. With my exposure meter I find what the lowest shadow values are, and I place them, usually, on Zone III. Next, I check the luminance of the outside foliage, presumably the brightest area, and I find that this will fall on Zone IX. This range implies a normal-minus-2 development time. It's complex at first, but it becomes sure and simple with practice. Often I might feel, 'I'm seeing it wrong', or 'I can't visualize it clearly.'

It's hard to turn down a picture, but there are some photographs about which you think at first glance, 'Oh, this is beautiful,' and then, when you start to visualize the print, you realize that it may not work.

Can you say something about this picture of a geyser – in particular some technical information along the lines of what we've just been talking about?

This is a photograph of the great geyser known as 'Old Faithful' because it blows precisely every sixty minutes. It's one of the features of Yellowstone National Park in Wyoming. It's never the same – steam pressure, wind, light conditions etc. keep the photographer very much on the alert. As we cannot guess how high the geyser will spout, a camera such as a Hasselblad is more functional than a view camera. But in this instance I wanted the rising front adjustment, and had just the right lens for my 7 × 5 view camera, so I settled for the larger instrument.

Old Faithful, Yellowstone National Park, Wyoming, c. 1940.

I think this image is very satisfactory. The values of the water and steam are very well held in the negative and print. I used Agfa Isopan film and a deep yellow (4X) filter. The bright water value was placed on Zone VI and normal-plus-2 development in Ansco 47 was used. Exposure was 1/200 of a second at f/22. By interpolation the bright water measured 1600 candelas per square foot luminance.

There was a young German photographer who was also shooting 'Old Faithful' at the same time and he said to me, 'Will you tell me what exposure you are giving?'

I said, 'I'm using Isopan film.'

And he said, '*Ja*, I have that here too – very good.'

Then I gave him 1/200 of a second at f/22 and he said, 'This is impossible. You will get nothing.'

I said, 'I think I will.' Of course he didn't know how I was going to apply the negative development, so I was four stops off according to him!

How do you feel about colour as opposed to black-and-white?

In colour you have a greater range in one way and a smaller one in another. You have not much control of values and a relatively short exposure range, but you can separate extremely subtle colours and control 'colour densities' by variations in exposure and filtration. Colours in nature are usually of low saturation, and quiet greens, browns and grey may respond much the same with black-and-white photography, but are luminous and distinct in good colour positives and negatives.

Orthochromatic film, which is sensitive to blue and green, is in many ways better than panchromatic film for nature photography. Practically all photographers use panchromatic film, which does have the added sensitivity to red. We can use a minus-red filter (Wratten, No. 44A) to achieve the effects of orthochromatic film. Photographers, including myself, are creatures of habit – and that's not always an advantage!

Talking about film, what do you like using for your black-and-white work?

Lately I've been using Kodak Tri-X Professional; Ilford FP4 – that's very fine; and Plus-X, which I find good. The makers give speed ratings that are usually too high for my taste, as I don't want to lose shadow detail. I suppose it helps the sale of film to advertise high speeds! I find that I get the best results by using film speeds about half the published recommendations. This business of 'pushing' speeds depends on rather extreme development of the negative. The lower values are lost, but the middle and high values come through with harsh contrast and severe grain.

How do you rate your portraits as opposed to your landscapes?

I did most of my portraiture before I had as much technique as I have now. Most of them were done in the 1930s.

Let's discuss some of them.

Yes. Foujita, the Japanese painter, came to my place in San Francisco and I photographed him using the first large flash bulbs – No. 75 aluminium foil-filled lamps in brushed aluminium reflectors. I had a formula. The main flash was about 4 feet from the subject and the secondary flash 6 to 10 feet distant, depending upon the light balance desired. I used a 5 × 4 view camera with a 12-inch Dagor lens, loaded with Kodak Super-Panchromatic film.

I seldom use flash now – I'm not very favourable to artificial light. The electronic flash lamps are superior, as the very short exposures they give are good for holding better high values of the subject.

Foujita, Artist,
San Francisco, 1933.

Georgia O'Keefe and Orville Cox, Canyon de Chelle, Arizona, 1937.

What about the Georgia O'Keefe picture, which is one of your most famous portraits, isn't it?

I made that picture with my 35mm Zeiss Contax at the Canyon de Chelle, Arizona, in 1937. There was a storm coming up. I was down there with my Comptax 3 and it was shot on Agfa Super Pan Supreme film. I think it's one of my best photographs, but unfortunately, while the 36-exposure roll was drying, it fell to the floor and this picture was in the section I stepped on! There were some very good pictures on that roll but this was by far the best. The scratch marks have been removed with the greatest care, but it remains difficult to make a fine print from that negative. Such is life! However, the image is a very popular one so I consider myself lucky.

And the portrait of Stieglitz? How was that taken?

Opposite: *Alfred Stieglitz at An American Place*, New York City, 1938.

I took it in his gallery, An American Place, in New York City. That was the radiator I sat on, waiting for him to see my pictures when I first met him in 1933. Boy – was it hot!

Fresh Snow, Yosemite
Valley, California, *c.* 1947.

How do you feel about selling your work?

I made the photograph of fresh snow in the Yosemite Valley into a three-panel screen for a client. I forget what I charged for it twenty years ago, but it now carries a very high value in the dealer-auction markets. None of this benefits me, but the high prices my work commands in the open market have had a good effect generally. Young photographers receive increased return on their work, and it's now possible for some to make a living from the sale of fine prints.

The picture was taken after a snowfall, in a very quiet light. The distant light is from far-off snowy cliffs. The forest is in heavy shade and I expanded the general contrast by extended development (normal-plus-1). The average luminance of the subject was placed on Zone V. I used a grade 3 paper for the print.

How do you manage your print sales?

My manager and I decided in 1975 that we had to do something – I was going bats! Orders were coming in for two of this and five of that and I was confined to my dark-room making random prints, to the detriment of fresh creative work. I wasn't getting much money for the prints at the time and it was hard to see a reasonable solution to the problem. My new manager, William Turnage, now Director of the Wilderness Society in Washington DC, had a wonderful idea. We announced that as of 31 December 1975 I would offer no further prints for sale. Dealers could place a large order before that date . . . and that was that! I received many more orders than I expected and it took me more than two years to fill them. It was an efficient solution to a difficult problem. The prints were far more consistent in quality because I could make a considerable number of the same subject, using the same run of paper. This avoided the inevitable adjustments which different batches of paper required. Since then I have made no prints for sale on the open market.

I made all the prints myself. Of course I have assistants to help in toning, washing, mounting and so on, but if I don't make the prints I cannot sign them. For every fine print made I assume that I must make at least five to gain the optimum one, and perhaps five more to overcome inherent paper defects, and accidents in handling, which can be many! Some defects don't show until the print is mounted. Such troubles can be quite discouraging.

Since you stopped making prints for sale how is your time mostly spent?

I've concentrated on my technical books and the preparation of my autobiography, and making prints for exhibits and monographs and special non-profit-making educational institutions. While I'm always very busy, I'm not under the same strain as in earlier years.

Are you still teaching?

Yes. I've been conducting my annual workshop in Yosemite since 1947, and it's become a traditional 'institution'. However, due primarily to my health – high altitudes and heat don't agree with me – the Ansel Adams Workshops have recently been moved to Carmel, where they will be held under the direction of the Friends of Photography, which is now the leading organization of its kind in the world. In the last decade we've expanded the workshop to include important instructors in various fields, and we've presented such luminaries as Arnold Newman, Yousuf Karsh and Olivia Parker.

Karsh is one of the people I shall be talking to very shortly. How would you characterize him?

Oh, Karsh is a great romantic character, a very fine man. Please give him my warm regards. He's very serious and I think would like to have been a philosopher – which he really is. He gave a talk to some students a few years ago at a workshop and they were practically in tears. He is the 'born again' photographer – dedication to the art is everything to him.

How would you sum up for your students what is most important in photography?

My last word is that it all depends on what you visualize. If you don't visualize a picture before you make it you might as well use a purely automatic camera. They are marvellous devices for their purposes but they cannot *create* for you, and that's not photography to me.

Eve Arnold

Eve Arnold is a photojournalist – perhaps the ultimate kind of photojournalist, since her work in the field of reportage includes interviewing and writing to complement her photographs. She was born in the USA, the daughter of Russian immigrant parents. When she was a young girl the chance gift of a camera from a friend awakened her interest in photography and for several years she experimented, taking photographs for her own pleasure.

During the war years she married a graphic and industrial designer, and while he was away she took a job in a photo-finishing plant, rapidly becoming first production manager and then plant manager. On her husband's return she gave up her job, had a child and for a brief time was a housewife, but she still considered herself a photographer and began once again to take pictures. She took a course at the New York School for Social Research where her work was admired by the great Alexei Brodovitch, art editor at *Harper's Bazaar*. Shortly afterwards she compiled a portfolio of photographs and sold some of them to *Picture Post*. In 1952 she joined the newly created photographers' co-operative, Magnum, of which she has since been an active member.

From that time onwards she has travelled the world as a photojournalist, working primarily for *Life* magazine and the *Sunday Times*, for whom she spent ten years as a contract photographer. Her work has appeared in most of the world's major magazines, such as *Stern, Paris-Match* and *Vogue*. In 1973 she wrote and directed a film on the harems of Arabia, entitled *Behind the Veil*. The BBC have produced a film about her work, called *The Unretouched Woman*. Her most recently completed project is a book on China.

Eve Arnold's photographs demonstrate her passionate interest in people, in the human and particularly the female predicament. She brings to her observations the sharply inquisitive, but at the same time uncensoring, eye of the journalist. She seeks to reveal inner meanings and truths by drawing attention to the unguarded moment when the subject has all but forgotten the presence of the camera, and she produces her vignettes unretouched, unposed, un-selfconscious.

'You can't make a great musician or a great photographer if the magic isn't there.'

Eve Arnold

Why did you take up photography?

I became interested because somebody gave me a camera. At that time I wanted to be a doctor and I was actually doing my pre-med. training, so at first I was just an amateur, shooting pictures for myself – and I had a small dark-room. Then two years before I joined Magnum I got together a portfolio.

Are you glad you chose photography rather than medicine?

I have never regretted my decision to become a photographer, because it's the most demanding thing I have ever done. There are so many dimensions to it, and I feel that in photography I'm using my creative ability to the absolute maximum.

Your pictures of movie stars are famous. Tell me something about this one of Marilyn Monroe.

Marilyn loved to have her photograph taken in a studio and I took this in Hollywood in 1960. She was very unhappy that day, but she cheered up when the session started. She had brought with her a retinue of assistants – hairdressers, make-up artists and so on. I had built a paper wall around us so that we wouldn't be observed during the session, but the team had cut peep holes in it. She knew exactly what was going on and she performed for her audience while pretending at the same time that she was playing to the camera.

There's an element of spontaneity – of reportage almost – in that picture, and of course that's the branch of photography for which you're known the world over. What to you is the most important aspect of reportage photography?

Firstly you have to be so much at home with your equipment that you can forget it exists. It's important, also, to develop a contact with your subject, and to do that you have to be sensitive, open to feelings and attitudes.

Do you find that very demanding?

As my work develops it certainly makes greater and more complex and far-reaching demands, both mentally and physically. I have to travel great distances, which presents all sorts of problems.

Has being one of the few women in photography hindered your career?

No, not really. Most of the time it's been a blessing. Women don't suffer from outright prejudice, although they sometimes tend to get overlooked. I've just received a Lifetime Achievement award from the American Society of Magazine Photographers. They've been giving the awards for thirty-five years, but this is the first time they have given it to two women – Louise Dahl-Wolfe and myself. Usually they give only one award, but this year they gave two. In my acceptance speech I said that I realized that this was not like the Arab system, in which two female witnesses are the equivalent of one male, but merely that after all these years of oversight they were trying to catch up as quickly as possible!

Would you call yourself a feminist?

I suppose I *am* a sort of half-baked feminist, and I do believe in the feminist movement, but I have to say that it's been an enormous help to me to be a woman. You see, men like to be photographed by women, and women don't feel that they have to carry on a flirtation, which they often do with a male photographer. However the physical side

Marilyn Monroe,
Hollywood, 1960.

24

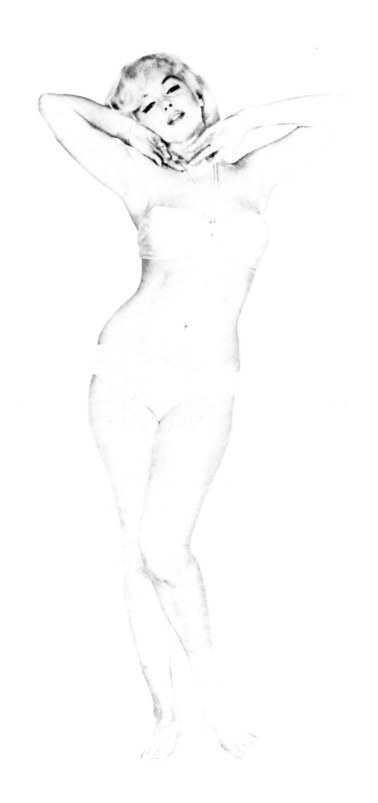

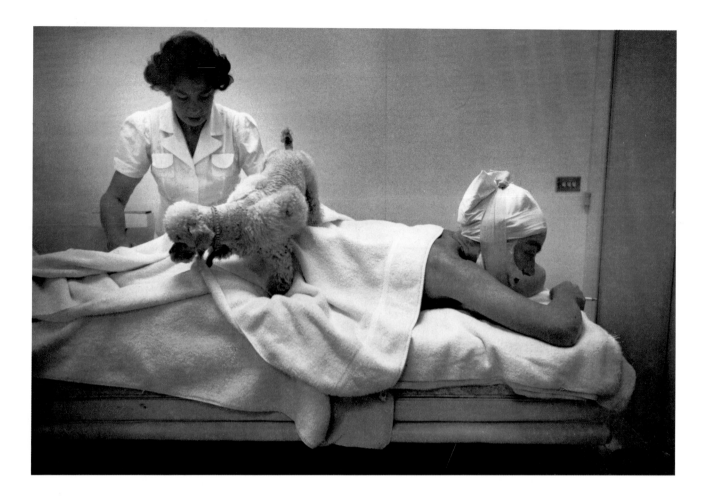

Joan Crawford,
Hollywood, 1959.

of photography – carrying bags, for instance – is a problem because I don't work with an assistant. I find that the tension produced just by revving myself up to get ready for a shoot is very wearing. A lot of psychic energy goes into my photography. I may take only two pictures and work for ten minutes, but when I wake in the morning I worry so much about checking the equipment and getting into the right frame of mind that by the end of the day I feel utterly drained. It was easier in the beginning, I think, when I worked solely in black-and-white and needed only a single camera. I feel that made a big difference. But, who knows, perhaps I've just forgotten how difficult it was then, too? Anyway, I'm certainly not prepared to put it down to old age.

What did Joan Crawford think of Marilyn Monroe? They were, after all, two very different women.

When I first met Joan Crawford she was really angry. She had just seen Marilyn at a studio and was scandalized by the fact that she didn't wear a girdle. I remember her saying that she was a disgrace to the industry. I had never thought of the film business being an industry before.

Did you always photograph Hollywood stars as you saw them?

I asked Marilyn Monroe how she saw herself and she replied, 'The Botticelli Venus'. I don't think she really knew what she meant because later, when I went to show her the pictures in New York, I gave her some Botticelli prints and put the 'Venus' on top. She didn't seem to recognize it at all.

Opposite: *Marilyn*
Monroe, 'Venus',
Hollywood, 1960.

26

You're now back in America after some years abroad. How does it feel?

The funny thing is that I seem to be going back with a new eye, seeing things afresh. America is such an exotic place, with so many regional differences, and that's the basis of what I'm doing now – I'm preparing a photographic account of my country's ethnic and cultural diversity.

Where in America did you shoot first?

Well, the American Indians were there first, so I thought it only a matter of courtesy to start with them, and I began on the Navajo Reservations.

Are you enjoying the assignment?

Yes, it's more of an adventure than work! Despite the fact that I've done an enormous amount of research, something is always turning up. I arrive somewhere and someone says, 'You can't possibly miss X out,' and so off I go again. It's a nightmare and a dream at the same time. It will take three years to complete, and it's such a daunting project both because every great photographer in the world has shot there and because everybody has their own idea of what America is. It's the most photographed country in the world, and so my book must be a very personal one in order to be original. America now has a feel of the fifties, of the McCarthy days, and yet it's not the same. On the one hand there's a kind of Fundamentalist thinking, but at the same time there's a lot of cultural activity too. It's difficult to know what to emphasize, because everything is so important to me. I'm working only in colour and that's posing a lot of problems. Without the confidence of my editor at Knopf and the success of my recent China project I wouldn't have dared touch this one. I may be about to fall on my nose, but at least I'll be seeing my home country with fresh, clear eyes. I'm simultaneously thrilled, appalled and delighted.

Has the book on China been a commercial as well as an artistic success?

Yes, it's done extremely well. It was published in Japanese, French and German, which is rare for a picture book. It was also chosen at the American Book Awards as the best designed book of the year, it won an award for the best cover and it was book of the month. Before the China project I was only known among other photographers – a photographer's photographer; they knew me from *Life* and the *Sunday Times*. Then all of a sudden people in the street had heard of me. That has been important to me in relation to the American project, because people point out to me things that they feel I should not miss, and I value their ideas. The exhibition of my Chinese pictures has been sponsored by Exxon, and will travel to museums throughout America for three years.

How did you arrange for a book to be made of your China trip – did you contact your publisher before or after your visit?

I had worked with Knopf on two other books, which were compiled from photographs that I had taken previously, and I discussed with my editor there the possibility of doing a book from scratch. I told him that I would be going to China for a magazine and asked him if he would be interested in a book. He said 'Yes', and that was it. The first time I went to China for the *Sunday Times* I stayed away from the book idea because I wasn't sure of the potential, but when I returned I stayed up literally for seventy-two hours and went through thousands of transparencies. That for me is the most nerve-racking moment in photography – wondering whether or not I have 'got it'. A friend called and insisted that I have a break, and so we went into the park on a beautiful spring day to relax and forget about work. We had a bottle of champagne. On the way back I heard my name called and it was my editor, visiting London. He had thought I was still in China. The next day he came to see the photographs, and the book was born. It was funny – everything just fell into place from start to finish. *Life* did a spread, *Paris-Match* covered it, *Stern* did sixteen pages, and the *Sunday Times* did two issues.

Much of your editorial work, like the China and America projects, consists of photographic essays. How much film would you use on one of these?

On China there were twelve thousand transparencies – it's not a lot. I shoot roughly five rolls a day. Also of course I do interviews, and that takes up a great deal of time. In China, too, I had agreed to teach; that was one of the stipulations made by the Chinese Government when they gave permission for the venture.

Did you find it disruptive?

It didn't bother me. They would send people from the official news agency and it was arranged like a workshop: we would have little sessions both before and after the shooting. They would stand on my toes to see what I was doing, to try to see the subject from my vantage point. The problem is that you don't know what you are going to shoot until you see it – you are always looking, searching – and having a lot of people trying to get as close to you as possible does not help!

What were the Chinese like as students?

They were always surprised by my choice of subject. They would point out the most banal situations, and often I didn't have time to explain why the subject they wanted me to photograph was uninteresting. I just pulled them along with me. They are still at the stage we were at in the fifties – lots of flash and Rolleiflexes. Though they do have wonderful cameras, such as Leicas and Hasselblads, they use bad Japanese film.

As a teacher, did you learn anything from those students?

On the last trip I was asked to talk to their editors, technicians and so on, and it helped to organize my own thinking a great deal. I began to realize that for years I had been doing all sorts of things that just weren't in the photographic textbooks – tricks of the trade, as it were. For example, if you want a portrait to appear really sharp you should focus on the eyes – *we* all know that it's a big disaster if the eyes are not sharp, but *they* didn't know. And they were horrified that I would often shoot – intentionally – directly into the sun. Little things like that.

Do you like commercial assignments?

I love the discipline that they demand. It teaches you great control, and you have to draw on all your technical knowledge. Working with art directors isn't always easy, and sometimes you seem to be just clicking a shutter, but the organization that must precede the shoot is very comprehensive. I tend to be a very organized photographer, even when doing editorial work. I like to organize everything first, so that during the actual shoot I can loosen up and 'play'.

For example, when I first went to China in 1979 I had to rely on the Chinese to show me things, but I'd done my homework and I knew exactly what I wanted to see. So I asked them about religion and their art schools and their millionaires, because I knew that some capitalistic principles had been re-established. They hadn't been asked those sorts of questions before and, having been asked, they were quite happy to oblige. If

I hadn't known what to ask for I would have seen all the usual sights that they had come to believe foreign journalists were interested in being shown. Preparation is the most important aspect of photojournalism – if you know what you want, most people will help you.

Opposite and above: *Marlene Dietrich*, USA, 1952.

China is about as far removed from your photographs of the glamour and superficiality of Hollywood as anyone could imagine. Marlene Dietrich is perhaps the epitome of the glamorous woman and yet in these pictures you appear deliberately to have deglamorized her – why did you want to do that?

In this series of pictures I wanted to show her as she really was – a working woman, quite different from the idealized version. Robert Capa got it right when he said, metaphorically, that my work fell between Marlene Dietrich's legs and the lives of migratory potato pickers!

How has it helped your career to be a member of Magnum?

Not many marriages last for thirty years! Magnum is a wonderful organization. There are about thirty of us, men and women with very different personalities, highly opposed points of view and different ethnic backgrounds. It doesn't work for everyone, and it works better for some than for others. For me it's a marvellous security blanket. The *Sunday Times* and Magnum have both acted as my base, from which I've been able to decide what exactly I want to do. That sort of security, and the freedom it gives, are a great privilege for any artist. Editorial reportage is wonderful, but it doesn't always pay the bills, so then Magnum might arrange for me to do some stills on a movie, or some industrial photography. I think I learned more from that kind of assigment than I did from doing editorial work.

What film do you use?

Tri-X for black-and-white, and I like Kodachrome for good colour balance. It's like playing roulette taking a slow film like Kodachrome on a trip, but I've been singularly lucky.

Do you use a lot of equipment?

No. I work with very little and I like to keep it simple. I use a 35mm camera. My feeling is that the eye sees with somewhere between a 40mm lens and a 50mm, so that's what I use. For portraiture I use 35mm, 55mm and 105mm lenses, and I have a zoom, 80–200mm. I don't use very much film on portraits.

During the last few years I've come to rely increasingly on an automatic Nikon. I stopped using a meter a long time ago, when I felt that I knew enough about light not to need it. However, an automatic camera is a real bonus to fall back on, especially when you are shooting colour.

Do you have any preference for working either in black-and-white or in colour?

I don't agree with all this nonsense about black-and-white photography being art and colour being commerce – that's lunacy. I'm greedy. I want to do everything. I want to shoot in black-and-white *and* in colour. I want to make films, and I want to write. There is no reason why you cannot do it all.

How do you consider the inter-relationship of writing and photography in your work?

I consider myself primarily a journalist, and I have never found the written word an intrusion as far as the photograph is concerned. I think one owes it to the viewer to provide the additional information.

Are you a technically minded person?

Not at all. I'm much more intuitive. For instance I never remember what exposure I have given a picture – I just don't care. I bracket a lot, taking different exposures of the same subject, and I take pictures in situations and light conditions in which people say it can't be done. Often it works.

I remember one time when I took a photograph of a black girl in a dark hallway lit only by a 60 watt bulb. It shouldn't have come out, but it did, and I was happy with the result which was used as a double-page spread. If I had gone by the book and strobed it I wouldn't have got the picture I wanted.

I play these games because it's fun to play. After all, it's only film, and when it works it can be wonderful. I like to work on the edges of the film. With very little light and very slow film you can get some great images. It's dicey, and it doesn't always work, but when it does the rewards are enormous. I would far rather do anything than play it safe. I'm a gambler by nature and I think it has paid off. Of course I lose a lot of images, and I use up a lot more film, but it's vital to get something that is entirely my own.

Presumably, then, it's impossible for you to try and define your techniques?

My techniques belong to me – you won't find them in any handbook! If I was to sum up, it would be true to say that I have no technique at all. It's all intuition. I've used myself and my equipment and the same method of working for so long that it's now second nature to me. I've forgotten about it, and now I would be hard pressed to explain it. I just concentrate on 'seeing'. I don't use a tripod, or artificial light. I can't analyze the technique – there is nothing except me.

It sounds extremely difficult to pass on such concepts to other people, and yet you taught when you were in China. How do you regard education in photography?

I don't think you can teach people to be good photographers. You can help to develop their power of 'seeing', but the moment you try to teach them you encourage them to be derivative. In the whole of Magnum I think that only Bruce Davidson had any formal photographic education. Without the 'seeing eye' the student can learn nothing from a teacher.

Let me give you an example. I was once hired by an art director to do some landscapes for a tourist agency. The man wanted to become a photographer and asked me all sorts of questions about cameras and techniques. When I was shooting he would stand beside me and try to take pictures from exactly my vantage point. At the end we compared photographs, and although he had been standing right beside me his pictures just didn't work. I don't know why, but they didn't. You can't make a great musician or a great photographer if the magic isn't there. That's why I'm not qualified to teach – what I've got is something that can't be passed on.

How do you feel that magic working for you, when you are taking pictures?

Even now when I work I may think that I've got something really great, only to find that I haven't. It's not something I can explain. Perhaps it's best to let the images speak for themselves – at the end of the day they are the only things that matter.

I love photography. Maybe mystery is too big a word, but it has that unknown quantity about it. One thing I find interesting, and have only recently started to think about, is that in that split second when I actually press the shutter absolutely anything can happen. Other images are forming that perhaps I hadn't noticed. In that moment in time a new figure might appear – one that I hadn't anticipated. So I always get what I see, but often something else as well. Sometimes colour foxes me, too. There can be marvellous surprises, and disappointments, but it's the element of the unknown that keeps up my interest in photography.

Photography is now a recognized form of art, and prints sell for large sums. What do you feel about that?

It's sad that a few elitist art pundits have made photography 'establishment', and I think that its commercialization in terms of collecting limited editions and signed photographs is pretentious. I would prefer photographs to be cheap and available to everyone – students should be able to buy them to stick on their walls. I once asked a dear friend of mine – a gifted photographer – what the difference was between the photography of the fifties and that of today. He replied 'That's easy. Photography in the fifties was about people. Now it's about photography.'

David Bailey

David Bailey was born in Leytonstone in 1938, but he was brought up in East Ham in the heart of London's East End. He became interested in photography when he was twelve, influenced by the Walt Disney and nature films he watched avidly in the local cinema. He borrowed his mother's Box Brownie and developed his own photographs in the cellar. When he was sixteen, his interest was stimulated again by the photographic images produced for the covers of jazz record albums.

'I've never been particularly interested in fashion – I was trapped into it in a way.'

He served with the Air Force in Singapore, where, at eighteen, he began to take photography seriously. On his return to England he joined the studio of fashion photographer John French, where he worked for eleven months. He continued his apprenticeship at Studio Five for a short time before embarking on his own professional career. In 1960 he was contracted to British *Vogue* where he immediately began to create for himself a formidable name as a fashion and portrait photographer. During the 1960s he became a seminal figure on London's social and artistic scene, as much a creator and arbiter of fashion as its recorder.

His international reputation has grown in recent years and he has worked for most of the world's major magazines. He has always been interested in the cinema and has made many commercial and documentary films. The latter include profiles of Andy Warhol, Visconti and Sir Cecil Beaton.

His one-man exhibitions have included those in London at the National Portrait Gallery in 1971; the Photographers' Gallery in 1973; and the Victoria and Albert Museum in 1983.

A complex personality, full of contradictions, Bailey today seems to be at a crossroads in his career as a photographer. Currently he is moving steadily away from the fashion photography which made him famous. He lives with his wife, the model Marie Helvin, near Regent's Park, and has just completed *Bailey's NW1*, a book of photographs taken in the run-down and neglected parts of that district of London, and which explore shape and pattern in such subject matter as drainpipes and derelict warehouses.

Would you say this picture of Mick Jagger is typical of your approach to portraiture?

It sums up what I was trying to achieve in portraiture in the 1960s. I was influenced by Penn at the time. He liked a lot of contrast in his pictures, so that was what I was aiming at. I was very young in those days and I didn't really know what I was doing. I still like white backgrounds, but I don't make them a hard and fast rule as I did then. I always end up breaking my own rules. The advantage of simple backgrounds is that they let you concentrate totally on the subject. In Mick's case it simplified everything and I think he comes across as the personification of the 1960s. I shot it on Tri-X film using a Rolleiflex camera. I also like to photograph people in their own environment.

How did you get into fashion photography?

I've never been particularly interested in fashion – I was trapped into it in a way. It seemed to me that John French and Tony Armstrong-Jones were the best photographers around, so I went for an interview with each of them. I was incredibly lucky because they both offered me a job. I took the one with John as it seemed cosier – they had three permanent assistants. Anyway Tony wanted to know if I could build sets and whether I was any good at woodwork. I told him I wanted to be a photographer, not a bloody carpenter!

Mick Jagger, London, 1964.

When I left John I worked for three months with Studio Five and then *Vogue* offered me a job as a staff photographer. In those days I wasn't that impressed by *Vogue*. The only difference between them and *Woman's Own* was that *Vogue* paid less! In fact I just didn't know anything about fashion photography. I told them that I'd like a contract with them, but I didn't want to work for them full-time. I think John Parsons, who was then the boss, was quite impressed by my arrogance because he offered me a year's contract and I worked for them until 1974.

But it drives me crazy when people say that I'm just a fashion photographer. Most of my published pictures aren't of women. I work every day and yet I seldom do fashion.

You've become as much a well-known personality as a well-known photographer.

Cecil Beaton was also both. The advantage is I can phone up anyone and they agree to sit for me. If I want to photograph a building, doors open up for me! But although my name was well known from the gossip columns my face wasn't recognized until I did the Olympus advertisements. When I wanted to take pictures of Lennon and McCartney, for instance, I didn't know either of them. I just telephoned and asked if I could photograph them. Now it's sometimes difficult to go out into the street to take pictures, and that's a limiting factor.

John Lennon and Paul McCartney, 1964.

Overleaf left and right:
Untitled, London, *c.* 1982.

37

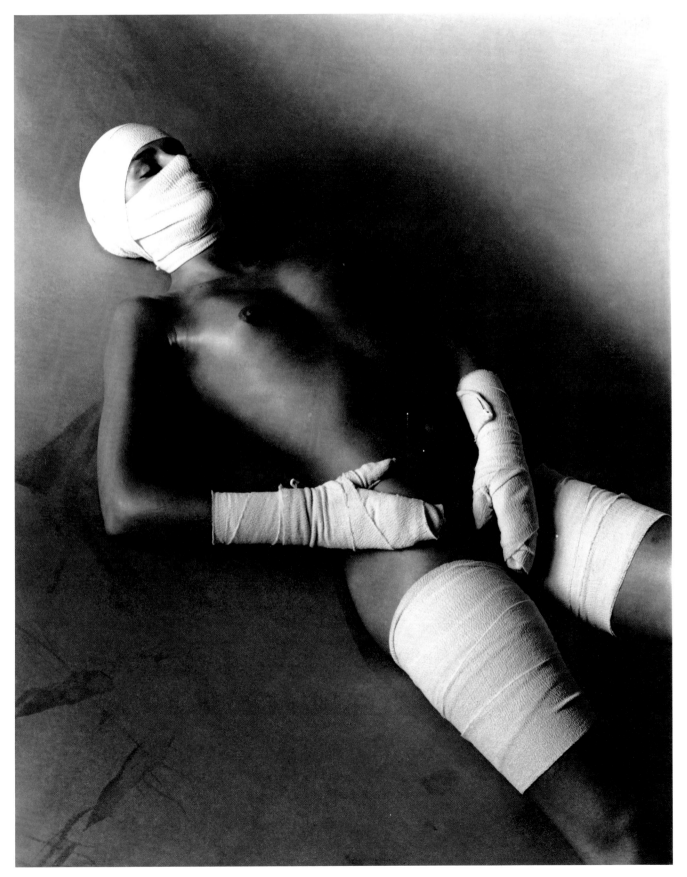

You've lived for short periods in America – have you ever thought of moving there permanently?

I don't really know. I'm always tempted. Certainly I'd be financially better off in New York. I'd be better off creatively as well, and more respected as a photographer. New York's a very visual city. The English disease is that they have no respect for their own talent and when they do recognize it they don't know how to cultivate it. The English are bitter and jealous of everyone else as well as being arrogant and lazy. Despite all that I don't see myself ever moving. I'd never want to sell my house here, although it's fine to live somewhere else for six months of the year. I need a permanent base.

Would you like to talk a little about these photographs – these pictures of the nude with the bandaged head and thighs, for example.

I'm really pleased with the series, and with these particular photographs. I shot them all in the last few weeks. They haven't been published yet and they won't be until my book comes out. In this photograph I achieved everything I'd intended. I thought about the session for a long time before I shot it and I think it's strangely surrealistic without being at all pretentious. For me it's a new way of looking at a naked girl, although I did something of the same sort with my picture of Marie wrapped in newspaper. I don't know why that struck such a strong chord in me. The photographs are certainly not remotely sexual and they're not about bondage either. The woman is a mystery – she belongs to everybody and yet to nobody. The printing enhances this feeling of mystery by being much darker than my usual prints.

One of the reasons I used the bandages was that I felt Helmut Newton had achieved a monopoly on stocking tops. That's silly, I know, but I felt I couldn't use them any more because they belonged to him. Not that I think there really is such a thing as a copy. If the artist has any talent, even an attempted copy will come across as completely different and original.

These pictures were shot on a 10×8 Deirdorf with an old Kodak lens.

You have an international reputation as being an inveterate collector of camera equipment. Is that true?

It's probably true that I have more *working* cameras than any other photographer in the world. I don't collect antique cameras. I love new equipment because I love to experiment. Each camera allows me to see life in a slightly different way and one of them is always right for a particular job. The mechanics of each camera dictate how the image is going to work. It's a bit like selecting a car for a particular task. You don't drive a Ferrari in the desert and you don't cover a riot in Brixton with a plate camera – you take a 35mm. I'm constantly testing different lenses, film and developer, and I know a great deal about technique although I don't always use it. It's nice to have it there and yet be able to ignore it.

What constitutes a 'good' picture for you?

I think most people underestimate the difficulty of taking a good picture. I'm a prolific photographer, but I'm thrilled if I like five of my own pictures out of a whole year's work. In the end when you take a picture everything counts and you can compensate in one area for deficiencies in another. For example I don't think Robert Frank's pictures would be any less good if they were sharper and less grainy. Cartier-Bresson shoots Tri-X on 35mm and it works, although his are not great technical pictures. He more than compensates with the subject matter.

Tell me something about these pictures of buildings.

I like these photographs of NW1. Recently I've shot a large number of them – more than I've done on one subject for a long time. I like the banality of the subject matter. Most people would pass these buildings every day of the week without really looking at them. There's no ornate cathedral wall, no Ralph Gibson abstract. Until you look closely, the buildings are banal and unimportant. But notice the way the shape of the lamp-post repeats itself in the chimney stack. The juxtaposition is accidental: they live next to each other by chance. In this way the photograph compares with an abstract painting. It's taken me a long time to arrive at this brick wall. It's a relief to know that after all that glamour there are ordinary normal things to photograph that can be made to look beautiful. These are the most important pictures that I've taken for a long time. I'm trying to capture the essence of the area in which I live, an essence revealed in the architecture. It's a beautification of banality.

Which camera do you like best?

I don't have any specific favourites. The job dictates it to some extent. For the *NW1* book I'd like to use a 10×8, but it's not practical to carry it around and so I'm using a 5×4. I always take a spare 35mm along on a session in case anything goes wrong.

What about lighting, lenses and film?

I don't take many lights with me on a session. I try to make do with what is available. I prefer banks of soft lights in the studio. I like the British Bowens system – it's a good unit and reasonably priced. I use Kodachrome for 'editorial'. Lately I've been using 5×4 Fujinon lenses quite a bit. They make a special soft lens which is very good for shooting colour and especially for beauty shots. I also like Schneider lenses.

Do you play around with the negative?

I don't double expose or anything like that. There's an old portrait trick I learned. If you turn the negative around the other way so that the model sees herself as she does in a mirror she's always pleased with the result. People are used to seeing themselves in a mirror – they never see themselves as others see them. I find if the girl is confident of the outcome, she's easier to work with. Of course you have to make sure she's not wearing buttons or a wedding ring.

Do you crop?

Seldom. I'm not against it in principle, but I prefer to crop the pictures by changing the format.

What is your ultimate ambition?

To be a better photographer and, believe me, it's difficult to progress all the time. It's a constant battle to create better images. I'm often not sure that I'll succeed.

Overleaf left and right:
NW1, London, 1981.

42

Bill Brandt

Bill Brandt was born in London in 1904 to British parents of Russian descent. His early life, spent largely in Germany, was characterized by ill-health, culminating in a bout of tuberculosis and four years in a Swiss sanitorium. Immediately after this, at the age of twenty-four, he went to Paris in 1929 to study with Man Ray. Abandoning his early ambition to be an architect, he had decided on a career as a portrait photographer.

Once in Paris, he was exposed to the work of the Surrealists which pervaded the artistic life of the city in the late 1920s. He was heavily influenced by their magazines and their novel way of using photographs, by the philosophy and work of the painter Chirico, and by Buñuel and Dali's film *Un Chien Andalou* (1928) and Buñuel's *L'Age d'Or* (1930).

Like Buñuel and Louis Aragon, Brandt was able to merge his Surrealist approach into a poetic realism; his main purpose was social comment, achieved through the accurate documentation of existing social conditions. In this he was closest to the contemporary Parisian photographers Brassaï and Atget, who captured the unguarded moment that revealed the essence of street poverty, the injustice and melancholy of city low-life, and the bitter-sweet humour and pathos of the brothel. Kertész, also in Paris at that time, favoured a similar style of photography.

In 1931 Brandt returned to England and started work on a book of photographs called *The English at Home*, published in 1936. This perceptive documentation of the customs and mores of English people from widely contrasting backgrounds is seen through the receptive and childlike eye of the stranger, for Brandt, despite his British birth, had spent little time in England. *The English at Home* was followed in 1938 by *A Night in London*, in which the sinister menace of the city at night is eloquently portrayed. Brandt was now working as a photojournalist, contributing work to the *News Chronicle*, the *Weekly Illustrated* (founded 1934), *Vogue*, *Lilliput* (founded 1937), *Picture Post* (founded 1938), and *Minotaure*.

In 1937 he toured the North of England, where he took moving and often disturbingly beautiful pictures of social deprivation and urban squalor. In 1938 he again turned his attention to London, producing the *Blackout in London* series, published in both *Lilliput* and *Life* magazine.

'The photographer must have, and keep in him, some of the receptiveness of the child who looks at the world for the first time, or of the traveller who enters a strange country.'

At the outbreak of the Second World War Brandt was employed by the Ministry of Information to photograph life in the air raid shelters and to document the damage to London's buildings. The former photographs were used for propaganda purposes, notably in America; the latter were useful in the setting up of the National Buildings Record, which appealed to the architecturally minded Brandt. In 1942 work for this organization involved him in a project to define the decay of the English country house. This was a theme that attracted him, not only because of its potential for sharp social comment on the divergent class structure of the masters and their servants who inhabited such houses, but also on account of the antiquarian melancholy of the overgrown landscapes that surrounded them. He found rich surrealistic value, as well as poetic beauty, in the forsaken gardens with their unspoken statements about the passing of the old order.

In 1943–4 the country house photographs were used by *Harper's Bazaar*, who, together with *Lilliput*, now commissioned him to take the portraits that the young Brandt had always dreamed of attempting. He produced the *Young Poets of Democracy* series which included Stephen Spender, Dylan Thomas and Laurie Lee. Later came portraits of Françoise Rosay, Robert Graves, J. H. Lartigue, E. M. Forster, Jean Dubuffet, Graham Greene, Magritte, J. B. Priestley and Henry Moore. Brandt's portraits are sombre and intense, often relying on props to reveal the essence of the subject. They are clever and sometimes rather stylized photographs, hinting that perhaps he did not always establish a close rapport with his subjects, preferring instead to rely on his artistic skill and faultless technique to reveal the sitter's personality rather than encouraging the sitter to unmask himself. From 1943 Brandt was commissioned to produce portraits for the American edition of *Harper's*. His international career was established.

In 1948 Brandt published *Camera in London*, continuing the themes of his earlier books, but his mind was already on other things. Neo-Romanticism demanded a return to the mysteries and splendours of the past as a reaction to social realism. The British landscape, picturesque, timeless, impressive and essentially English, was a suitable subject. Brandt suggested a series of photographs depicting Hardy country, and the resulting photographs of Hardy's Wessex secured him a position among the very greatest landscape artists.

The zenith of his achievement in landscape photography came with the publication in 1951 of *Literary Britain*, in which photographs of landscapes are used to evoke literary associations. These brooding masterpieces, heavy with suspense and a mysterious sense of transcendental dread, are magnificent in their elemental force. Dramatic contrasts, clever use of shadow, a constant awareness of geometrical shape, together with a consumate skill in the observation of cloud and mist, are the salient features.

If Brandt had been moving away from social comment in his landscapes, away from poverty and pessimism, the process was completed in his nude photographs. The link with the landscapes is clear and the nude form is treated as if it *was* a landscape. At first photographed in bare rooms, later, in the early 1950s, transferred to the seashore, the nudes actually become a part of the landscape, arms, legs, hands and feet merging with the rocks and stones in perfect harmony. Unusual vantage points and strange perspectives project that surreal quality for which Brandt had always strived. In these voluptuous nudes the harrowing truths of the early photographs are at last submerged. Here is the synthesis of his art, and in 1961 the results of fifteen years' work were seen in the brilliant *Perspective of Nudes*.

Such a departure had demanded a new scientific approach. Brandt had discovered an old brass mahogany stand camera with no shutter, its wide-angle lens focused on infinity, its aperture a simple pin hole. Its advantage was that Brandt was unable to see

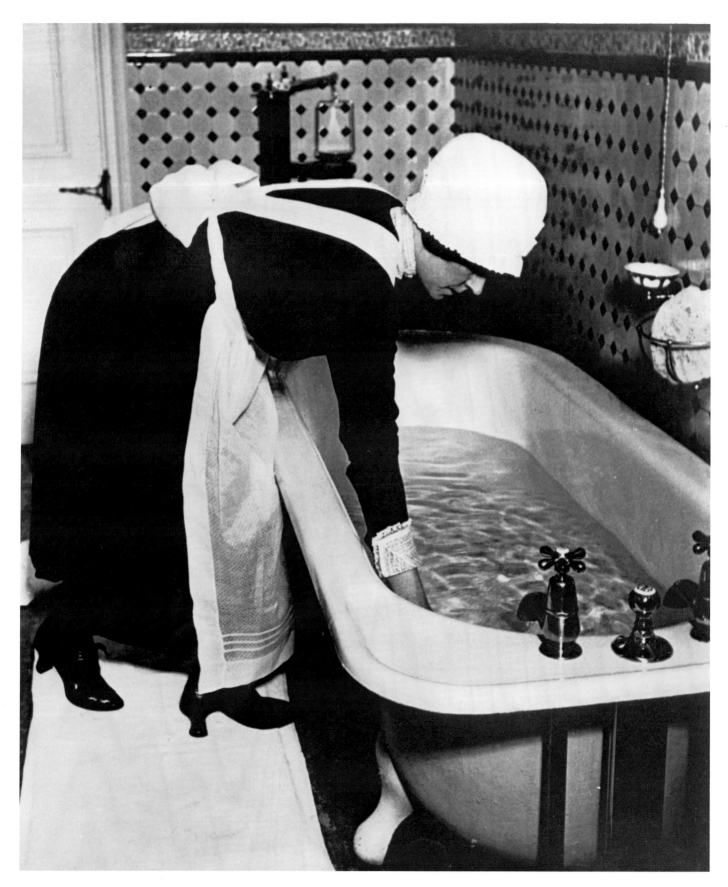

the image on the ground glass screen. The camera itself had to do all the work: Brandt was merely the operator, the blind orchestrator of the photograph. The results are unique because they are revealed by the mechanical eye of the camera. They could not be conceptualized in advance. The camera 'sees' with the eye of a child, unprejudiced, untutored, unarranged – the fundamental technique of Surrealism.

Brandt exhibitions have included *Arts et Métiers Graphiques*, Paris, 1938; and shows at the Museum of Modern Art, New York, in 1969; and the Hayward Gallery, London, in 1970. His work is in collections at the Museum of Modern Art, New York; the Victoria and Albert Museum, London; the International Museum of Photography, Rochester, New York; the Bibliothèque Nationale, Paris; and many others.

Today Brandt lives with his wife in London and is still at work, the undisputed old master of English photography. Surrealist, social commentator, revealer of landscapes and the female form, he is in photography a man apart – a hero of the medium – whose artistic skills few have equalled.

Bill Brandt has lived in his Campden Hill flat for the past twenty years. He is a tall, gaunt, graceful man with a quiet, courteous manner; his soft, gentle voice has the hint of a German accent. His flat is bare of photographs – two Victorian paintings hang on the wall, a china doll sits on one of the chairs. The windows overlook the square and Brandt talked of the beauty of the chestnut trees, looking forward to the time when the leaves and blossoms would block out the surrounding buildings. He seldom works at home, preferring to photograph people in their own environment.

Brandt dislikes talking about his work and is reticent about discussing his techniques, especially his philosophy of photography. He politely but firmly refused to let me use my tape recorder and tended to deflect most questions about his photography. He is uninterested in recent scientific developments, saying that apart from his famous mahogany stand camera he now used only a Hasselblad, rejecting colour, and preferring to be photographed himself in black-and-white. He is currently working on the compilation of a book of his portraits, doing all his own printing as always.

For Brandt's direct comments on his work we referred to his personal introduction to his book Camera in London *(1948). This is the only occasion that he has put his thoughts about photography on record.*

When he returned from Paris, Brandt found his inspiration in the streets of London.

I've tried to capture some of its magic, something of the spell that it can work as one strolls through deserted streets on a quiet summer evening, something of the brooding fantasy hidden in its stones.

His work never gets far from stones: the awesome majesty of Stonehenge, the cobbles of Halifax, or the seashore pebbles on which his later nudes recline.

I always had an interest in architecture, so early in my career I photographed buildings. But my pictures did not satisfy me. I looked upon the work then as the recording of buildings, and as records my pictures were adequate. Yet they lacked something, some quality which I could not name, and vaguely felt would have given me pleasure. So I turned to landscapes. I am not sure why I did this, because, although I appreciate the beauty of the countryside, I have never thought of myself as a lover of nature. And yet here was a seeming paradox. Something in these pictures of landscapes pleased me, although I had no great interest in the subject matter. Slowly a new development took place. Almost without my realizing it stonework began to encroach upon my landscapes. Little by little, a milestone, the tombs in a churchyard, a distant house in a park, until there was a fusion – not consciously sought by myself – of the subject that

Parlour Maid Preparing a Bath before Dinner, London, 1930s.

interested *me* and that indefinable something which gave me pleasure: aesthetic or emotional, call it what you will.

It was essential for Brandt that the subject matter of the photograph contained within it something of special interest to him – the stone monuments insinuated into the landscapes, the social comment contained within the pictures of deprivation and urban poverty, the nude moulding into the stark geometry of the bare room, the Victorian character of E. M. Forster's room expanding the novelist's personality and throwing the sitter into sharper relief.

I believe that it is important for the photographer to discover what he wants to photograph. Unless he finds out what it is that excites him, what it is that calls forth at once an emotional response, he is unlikely to achieve his best work. For me it was not easy – simply because my response was so much a matter of instinct that consciously I could not formulate it. In fact I did not try to do so. I now have, through experience, a more conscious knowledge of what it is that excites me – or would it be more exact to say of what does *not* excite me? Yet instinct should be a strong enough force to carve its own channel. Too much self-examination or self-consciousness about it or one's aims may, in the early stages, be a hindrance rather than a help.

If his instinct did not guide him, either consciously or subconsciously, a photographer might work for years without experiencing the excitement of creative work with his camera. To discover what it is that quickens his interest and emotional response is particularly difficult for the photographer today because advances in technical equipment have made it possible to take such a wide variety of subjects under such varying conditions that the choice before him has become immense in its scope. The good photographer will produce a competent picture every time, whatever his subject. But only when his subject makes an immediate and direct appeal to his own interests will he produce work of distinction. It may be that he already has some existing interest – in lighting, people's expressions, science – which will determine his choice, because where his interests are there will his seeing eye be also.

But if, for Brandt, the photographer must have an interest in his subject, he must also develop the power to 'see' his subject in a special way, and, through his work, show others how to do the same. This, he maintains, is a fundamental aim of photography.

The photographer must first have seen his subject, or some special aspect, as something transcending the ordinary. It is part of the photographer's job to see more intensely than most people do. He must have, and keep in him, some of the receptiveness of the child who looks at the world for the first time, or of the traveller who enters a strange country. Most photographers would experience a certain embarrassment in admitting publicly that they carried within them a sense of wonder, yet without it they would not produce the work they do, whatever their particular field. It is the gift of seeing the life around them clearly and vividly as something that is exciting in its own right.

I believe this power of seeing the world as fresh and strange lies hidden in every human being. In most of us it is dormant. Yet it is there even if it is no more than a vague desire, an unsatisfied appetite that cannot discover its own nourishment. I believe it is this that makes the public so eager for pictures. Its conscious wish may be simply to get information. But I think the matter goes deeper than that. Vicariously, through another person's eyes, men and women can see the world anew. It is shown to them as something interesting and exciting. There is given to them again a sense of wonder.

This should be the photographer's aim, for this is the purpose that pictures fulfil in the world as it is today – to meet a need that people cannot, or will not, meet for themselves. We are most of us too busy, too worried, too intent on proving ourselves

Nude, March 1952.

right, too obsessed with ideas to stand and stare. We look at a thing and believe we have seen it. And yet what we see is often only what our past experiences tell us should be seen, or what our desires want to see. Very rarely are we able to free our minds or thoughts and emotions and just see for the simple pleasure of seeing. And as long as we fail to do this, so long will the essence of things be hidden from us.

Brandt maintains that the photographer must try to avoid preconceived ideas and rely instead on developing receptive powers that allow him to experience the subject's 'atmosphere'.

I found atmosphere to be the spell that charged the commonplace with beauty. And still I am not sure what atmosphere is. I should be hard put to define it. I only know it is a combination of elements, perhaps most simply and yet most inadequately described in technical terms of lighting and viewpoint, which reveals the subject as familiar and yet strange. I doubt whether atmosphere, in the meaning it has for me, can be conveyed by a picture of something which is quite unfamiliar to the beholder . . . while if it does not show the subject in a new light the photograph is dead, a record on the flat print and no more.

Everyone has at some time or other felt the atmosphere of a room. If one comes with a heightened awareness, prepared to lay oneself open to their influence, other places, too, can exert the same power of association. It may be of association with a person, with simple human emotions, with the past or some building looked at long ago, or even with a scene only imagined or dreamed of. This sense of association can be so sharp that it arouses an emotion almost like nostalgia. And it is this that gives drama or atmosphere to a picture.

When I have seen or sensed — I do not know which it is — the atmosphere of my subject, I try to convey that atmosphere by intensifying the elements that compose it. I lay emphasis on one aspect of my subject and I find that I can thus most effectively arrest the spectator's attention and induce in him an emotional response to the atmosphere that I have tried to convey.

Brandt relies on instinct for his composition, believing that slavish adherence to textbook rules results in boring photographs. Printing and enlarging are important and must be done by the photographer. He admits, however, that the production of an effective photograph is a hit-or-miss process and that one must learn by trial and error.

Yet when all is said and done I do not really know how I take my pictures. I photograph the subject as I see it. Perhaps something lies in being ready to see the picture. Just as there is a right moment in action photography so other subjects, too, have moments when they are seen in their most interesting and exciting aspects. A photographer must be prepared to catch and hold on to those elements which give distinction to the subject or lend it atmosphere. They are often momentary chance-sent things: a gleam of light on water, a trail of smoke from a passing train, a cat crossing a threshold, the shadow cast by a setting sun. Sometimes they are a matter of luck; the photographer could not expect or hope for them. Sometimes they are a matter of patience, waiting for an effect to be repeated that he has seen and lost, or for one that he anticipates. Leaving out the question of the deliberately posed or arranged photograph, it is usually some incidental detail that heightens the effect of the picture, stressing a pattern, deepening the sense of atmosphere. But the photographer must be able to recognize instantly such effects.

Brandt hardly ever takes photographs except on assignment, finding that the necessity of fulfilling the contract concentrates the mind wonderfully. He seldom carries a camera with

him when he is not working and is able to switch off completely from photography when not actually doing it. He likes to prepare himself for assignments by visiting the place to be photographed beforehand, to experience its atmosphere. On a portrait session he sometimes takes along a companion to talk to the sitter.

I find it slightly distracting to have someone watching me as if I might spring upon him and extract a tooth at any moment. I am left free to gather my impressions of the people and their surroundings and to make up my mind where, and how, to arrange them together to get what I want.

He is not trigger-happy – he gets on average three usable prints from a twelve-negative film. He works with a Weston exposure meter and stops down to the smallest aperture possible. He dislikes synchronized flash and never uses filters. He works slowly and deliberately.

If there is any method in the way I take pictures, I believe it lies in this. See the subject first. Do not try to force it to be a picture of this, that or the other thing. Stand apart from it. Then something will happen. The subject will reveal himself.

Opposite: Untitled, Belgravia, London, 1953.

Overleaf left: *Coal Searcher Going Home to Jarrow*, 1930s.

Overleaf right: *Francis Bacon Walking on Primrose Hill*, London, 1963.

Harry Callahan

Harry Callahan is a gentle, straightforward man who values simplicity, and is opposed to intellectualization and to analysis of his motives in photography. Nevertheless he is articulate and informative when talking about his work, and has been a distinguished teacher of photography.

He was born in Detroit in 1912. His school record was unimpressive: 'I was no good as a student,' he said. 'I never paid any attention. I used to concentrate for a while and then my mind would wander to other things.' In 1936 he attended Michigan State University for three semesters to study engineering, and in the same year he married Eleanor Knapp. She was to be the inspiration for many of his greatest photographs and a source of strength and support throughout his life.

In 1938, with his friend Todd Webb, Callahan took up photography as a hobby. He joined a camera club called the Detroit Photo Guild in 1940, and in 1941, after attending a series of lectures given by Ansel Adams, he decided to make photography his career. He was twenty-nine.

Callahan produced some of his best work in the early 1940s, making elegant, austere, technically correct images of nature, whose economy of style and geometric form achieved the simplicity of effect that he sought. Sunlight on water, reeds on a pond or a leaf in the snow were typical of the natural subjects of his work, in contrast to the more grandiose landscapes of his mentor, Ansel Adams. During 1944–5 he worked as a processor in the photographic laboratory at General Motors, and at about this time he started to work in colour.

In 1946 he took up a teaching post at the Chicago Institute of Design, for which he was interviewed by Moholy-Nagy. When asked by Moholy-Nagy about his proposed methods as a teacher, he replied, 'When they see my work, they will know what I mean.' He was to live in Chicago until 1961, becoming a Head of Department at the Institute in 1949. During these years his friends Hugo Weber, Mies van der Rohe, Aaron Siskind and Edward Steichen exerted strong influences on him which had important implications for his career. Steichen's recognition of his artistic talent, in particular, encouraged him greatly and led to his work being extensively exhibited at the Museum of Modern Art in New York, where Steichen was Director of the Department of Photography.

'Photography is a modern medium. Like the roof of the Sistine Chapel, it should be for all the people.'

In 1956 Callahan was awarded a Graham Foundation grant which enabled him to spend fifteen months taking photographs in Europe, especially around Aix-en-Provence in France. He left Chicago in 1961 for the Rhode Island School of Design, where he was appointed Professor. He was awarded a Guggenheim Fellowship in 1973, and two years later a National Endowment for the Arts, both of which enabled him to travel widely in Mexico and South America. The Center for Creative Photography in Tucson, Arizona acquired archival material on Callahan in 1975.

His one-man exhibitions have included shows at the Light Gallery, New York, in 1974, 1976, 1978 and 1980; the Museum of Modern Art, New York, in 1952, 1961, 1967 and 1976; the Art Institute of Chicago, in 1951; and the Kansas City Art Institute, in 1956. He has also participated in numerous group exhibitions.

———•———

How did you become involved in photography?

One of my wife's cousins showed me his film camera. I thought it was extremely beautiful and I went to a shop to buy one. However it cost an awful lot of money, so in the end I bought a Rolleicord.

Might you have been a film cameraman or director if you had had the money then?

No. I have shot movies, but still photography allowed me to be myself – to do my own thing. I could never have worked as a member of a team, and I just don't have the temperament to be a director. I need to be alone.

Despite that, you used to go off with Todd Webb to photograph Colorado and Estes Park. Did you enjoy those trips?

No, but not just because I preferred to be alone. When Ansel Adams first came to Detroit he showed me pictures that he'd taken in his own back yard. This set me free. I thought, 'I don't have to go to great National Parks, or find great architecture, to make a good photograph. I can find one within ten feet of myself.' The real reason that I didn't like my pictures of Estes Park was that I didn't see anything there that I wanted to photograph. The spectacular mountains just didn't interest me – not that I'm against anybody else shooting them. I've had that feeling ever since. I'm the opposite of Ansel in a way, and I always preferred his other photography – the portraits, for instance.

Was his influence on you more spiritual than technical?

It was the whole works. Ansel came along at a very crucial stage in my life when I had lost my religion – it had always been very important to me, and it left a deep void. I'd always wanted to contribute to humanity, but had no outlet. When I saw Ansel's prints it provided the answer for me. I saw it at once, and everything came together for me at that point.

Luckily I had enough technical skill to benefit from his teaching, so I asked him as many questions about technique as I possibly could – everything from developer to paper and film. He told me to use ABC Pyro film developer, Isopan film and Amidol print developer, for example.

Later it was a big thing for me to break away from his techniques. For Ansel, texture and fine detail were vital. When I began to eliminate tone and show only lines in my landscape photographs it represented the breaking of a tradition for me. I had thought it was a sin not to get texture into your pictures, not to print on No. 5 paper rather than No. 2. That's how powerful his influence was.

Ansel used to talk of Stieglitz as if he was a God. Later I realized that Stieglitz was just a cranky old man. I guess that's all part of growing up. Ansel would talk in depth about the colours of different paper and I could never see the importance of it – but because he used a certain paper, I would use it too. That went on for several years, but I don't care about any of that now.

So you're not interested in the scientific side of photography?

I was never any good at it. I don't know anything about the chemistry of photography. In fact I know even less about it now than I did before. I only know how to make a print the way I like it to look. All I have ever wanted to do was to make things more simple.

You seem to have achieved that increasingly with your images over the years.

Yes. It's developed unconsciously and come as something of a surprise. For instance my landscapes are just some sand, whereas Ansel's are splendid mountains. That's the real excitement of photography: things come out of you that you never knew were there.

eanor, Chicago, 1949.

Harry Callahan

Eleanor, Port Huron, 1954.

You talk as if photography has enormously enriched your life and taught you more about yourself.

Before photography nothing was important to me. I was merely existing with no purpose at all. Now I use the medium to express the things that are happening in my life. As my life changes, the work reflects it. It seems that life and photography must be closely related.

You have taken many photographs of your family – your nudes of Eleanor have been especially successful.

I don't know why nudes have been so important to me. It was lucky that Eleanor was so co-operative in posing for me, because I had to have a feeling for the subject. Just any nude wouldn't have done. I took nude pictures of her from the forties to the sixties, but then she went back to work and that was the end of it.

I particularly like the 1954 photograph of Eleanor at Port Huron.

There was another version of this photograph on the contact sheet that I like very much, but other people preferred this one. Perhaps if I hadn't just let the matter go, things might have been different. This picture is widely known now.

Tell me about this photograph of Eleanor standing by the window.   *Eleanor*, 1948.

I put her by the window because I wanted to shoot straight into the light. I used a 10×8 camera and exposed it for twenty seconds. There is some movement, but it doesn't matter. After the war we were living in a big room which had been the ballroom of an old house – the landlord rented out the rooms and we got the ballroom. It was good for taking photographs, and I took a lot with Eleanor there.

What events in your life have most influenced your work?

First marriage, and the birth of our daughter. And I think being invited to teach at the Institute of Design in Chicago opened all sorts of doors in terms of the art world. Then, out of the blue, I got a scholarship. We went to live in the South of France, and with each development my life opened up more. And then I went to work with Moholy-Nagy.

What was he like?

He was a brilliant person – good at everything, including the manipulation of people – and a great artist. I only knew him for the six months before he died, but he worked the living daylights out of me.

How did his influence on you compare with that of Ansel Adams?

He struck me as being a much bigger man than Ansel. I very much respect Ansel, but I don't care for his approach, which I find too narrow. In contrast Moholy was a man with broad vision. Ansel has achieved a great deal and elevated the status of photography, but even an idiot could understand his pictures. Moholy was an extremely erudite man who could talk well on any subject.

Would you agree that some of your early collages influenced certain painters, like Warhol and Richard Hamilton?

Who is Richard Hamilton?

A British painter who used fashion magazine photographs in some of his prints of the late 1950s.

I did those collages in 1956, and I think that several artists, working independently, can share the same stream of consciousness without knowing it. For instance I was working once on a series of pictures and a friend of mine, who came to the Institute of Design, was making sculptures in the same way. On another occasion I was using strobe in conjunction with all kinds of camera movement in an effort to break away from the static, standard stuff. When I saw Jackson Pollock's pictures with all that dripping paint it struck me that it was basically the same idea.

Why didn't you use your own photographs in your collages?

I had seen an article in *Life* magazine on slavery and I wanted to express my view in some way. I started cutting out the photographs, pinning them up and photographing them. Unfortunately I didn't get very far with that idea, because I ran out of slave pictures. Instead I got hold of a lot of fashion magazines, like *Harper's Bazaar*, and cut out pictures of beautiful models. I have no idea what my motivation was. I just did it.

When you are shooting what might be considered reportage photographs do you worry about invasion of privacy?

Yes. I'd find it difficult to do a portrait, for instance, even if I'd been asked to do it by the sitter. I'd feel very self-conscious, and I think I'd make the other person self-conscious too.

Do you use a plate camera now?

No – I use 35mm. I like a single lens reflex. I first used 35mm in 1941 when I had a Contax and a Leica. In those days they didn't even come close to the clarity of a 10×8. At that time, too, you thought of yourself as being a more serious photographer if you used a 10×8.

Do you use artificial light much?

No. I used strobe in the early days, but it didn't synchronize well then and I gave it up as a bad job. I got disgusted with it. I never trusted flash.

Have you ever shot 'snaps'?

Not as such, but a lot of pictures of my wife and daughter that were published in *Callahan* were inspired by the idea of the snapshot. I wasn't actually intending to take a 'snap', but when I saw the result I thought, 'That's an interesting way to take a photograph.'

Have you ever used a Polaroid?

No, never. I feel there's something wrong there – you've got to do more than that. I guess it has a purpose, although I don't know what it is.

What type of film do you use?

For a start colour – I stopped using black-and-white in 1976. For 35mm I use Kodachrome 64, and on the few occasions when I use a $2\frac{1}{4}$ square camera, it's Ektachrome. I prefer 35mm. It's the most liberating camera in existence.

What made you change to colour?

Well, I always did do colour. One of its advantages is that I don't have to process, which saves a lot of time and lets me get on with taking photographs. For my major show at MOMA I had to do a lot of printing, and got way behind.

You sell your prints through the Light Gallery. Were you surprised when they approached you?

I was surprised because I didn't expect my work to sell. It was a great relief to be rid of the financial burden. The first print, involving the dye transfer, is very expensive. The Light Gallery saw some colour slides and had a whole selection of prints done. Luckily they sold well. I would have been scared to have $50,000 worth of prints made without knowing for certain that they'd sell. Now that sales are established I don't have to worry. One of the best things about being with a gallery was that I was invited to other artists' exhibitions. The sale of my own work was a bonus.

Ansel Adams is leaving all his negatives to the Center for Creative Photography in Tucson, Arizona. Will you do the same?

Yes. They were the people who first started printing my colour. The President of the University is mad keen on photography, and he got a National Endowment for the Arts and raised money to exhibit my work. The idea in starting these archives was to get the work of the very best photographers. Ansel Adams was the first artist to be approached. Frederick Sommer, Aaron Siskind and Wynn Bullock were also involved. They paid us a lump sum for the use of our work for ten years, which enabled me to retire from teaching. Unfortunately, since then I don't think that the Center has had any money to buy anybody else's work, but they have other devices that they can use instead. For instance, they acquired Eugene Smith's work by getting him to teach at a very high salary.

Ansel Adams feels strongly that students should be free to print from his original negatives so that they can make their own original interpretation of his work. What do you think about that?

I hadn't heard of that scheme before, but I don't particularly care one way or the other. I guess the Center would keep the master print and the student would have to match it. Probably a lot of Ansel's prints are made by someone else. Many photographers don't make their own prints, but make a master and get someone else to copy it. Kertész is a good example – he hasn't made his own prints for years. I think he gets some sort of unpleasant reaction from the chemicals. Cartier-Bresson has never made his own prints. Possibly Ansel exposes them all and then gets an assistant to take over, after telling him what to do. I've always printed my own pictures, but that's mainly because I don't like having assistants around.

When do you feel you produced your best work?

I've enjoyed the last few years most of all. In terms of my work I think the images were better in the past, but life itself has become easier for me. Experience piles up. In my early days I thought I worked a lot, but on looking back I realize I wasn't that prolific. As you grow older you get to know yourself, and what you are trying to achieve, and you don't go through all those agonizing periods of self-doubt. I used to monkey around with my prints a lot – a little less exposure here, a little more there – and then I discovered that it's better to get each exposure normal, as simple as possible.

Do you ever discover images taken in the past that have been overlooked in some way?

Yes. Nobody liked a certain picture of my wife Eleanor, taken around 1947, until Szarkowski used it on the cover of the *Callahan* book. I myself had always liked it.

How do you like to show your work?

I suppose my preference is for books. Certain photographers prefer to show their images large, but I think all mine can be shown small. Photography is so young that nobody knows the best way to view it yet. Some people have talked of making a limited edition, of destroying the negative and all that junk. I'm against that. Some day I might just find that a particular picture looks better as big as that wall. Photography is a modern medium. Like the roof of the Sistine Chapel, it should be for all the people.

Do you miss teaching?

No, I always wanted to get out. However I do feel rather ambivalent about it. Because I love photography so much I was a successful teacher, although I never knew what or how to teach. It's the same with my photography. I just don't know why I take the pictures I do.

Do you ever have a problem deciding which direction to take in photography?

I knew that I wanted to take pictures more than anything else, and I knew that I didn't want to do it commercially because my personality wouldn't allow me to do it that way. When I got bored with landscape I changed to buildings. Instead of waiting for inspiration I changed my subject matter. Every change I've made has been a super-challenge.

Did you ever want to paint?

I remember going to MOMA in 1942 to see Stuart Davis's abstractions, and through Stieglitz I was introduced to the paintings of Georgia O'Keefe. As a result of that I wanted to make abstractions. But although I was influenced by painting I never wanted to do anything else except photograph. I think some of my multiple exposures are a result of my interest in abstract painting. I would like to have painted, but only because I had friends who painted and I wanted to be on the same wavelength as them.

When you make your multiple exposure pictures do you use only a single negative?

Yes. I don't mind someone else putting two negatives together, but I don't do it myself. You have to understand that when I started in photography there was nobody else except Ansel Adams, Stieglitz and Steichen. There was no one else to relate to at all, and to that extent I was a purist. At the time Ansel had got me interested in music and I was thinking a lot about it, in a very pure way. As part of that purity I believed that there should be only one negative. Then, if anyone else were to print my pictures there would be no problems.

Eleanor, c. 1947.

Eleanor, Chicago, 1953.

How did you shoot the multiple exposure on Eleanor in the 1953 photograph?

I took a triple exposure on a single negative. The first, using back lighting, was of an egg. The next exposure was a silhouette of Eleanor, using a floodlight in a reflector. The third was of a landscape. Her body had to coincide with the branches, which was why it was a silhouette. I used the same exposure for each shot so that each image would have equal strength. The camera was a 5 × 4 Linhof.

Do you crop your pictures?

No, hardly ever. You see most people proof their pictures, but I never proof mine. I just put them in the enlarger, look at them, and if I like them I print. Making a proof, cropping it and then putting it away with the negative would have been the simple way, I suppose, but I just never thought of it.

How many successful images do you hope to achieve in a single year?

Maybe I will end up with half a dozen. I've just had a new visual idea in the past couple of days. During the two weeks that I'm here in London I'll work on that solidly, shooting most days. Probably I'll get only one picture out of it.

This new idea of yours involves shooting into shop windows. What lenses and cameras will you be using for that?

I have a couple of Canon SLRs and I'll be using lenses ranging from 17 to 50mm.

How much film do you expect to expose in these two weeks?

Four or five rolls in the morning and the same in the afternoon. Half of the time I'm just experimenting, but I feel that the mere snapping of the shutter involves some kind of relevant decision, which in turn leads on to some other decision.

What advice would you give to a young student of photography?

If I were to venture advice I'd hate myself for it. There are so many avenues to explore. Some people need to sit around thinking for a month before they can go out and take a good picture. Others have to shoot all the time. It's so hard to figure photography out – you can only find the answers for yourself.

Chicago, 1960.

Louise Dahl-Wolfe

Louise Dahl-Wolfe was born in San Francisco in 1895, the daughter of a marine engineer. In 1914 she went to the San Francisco Institute of Art intending to become a still-life painter. She studied design and colour under Rudolph Schaeffer at the Institute and says of her five years there, 'On thinking over my long career in photography I've arrived at the following conclusion – that if there were any successes they were due to the knowledge that I gained there . . . . It's easy to learn the technique of the camera on your own, but there I learned the principles of good design and composition. Drawing from the nude in the life class made me aware of the grace and flow of line and of the differences between male and female poses. This was important for fashion photography.'

In 1914 she met Anne Brigman, the photographer of nudes, and began to experiment with photography herself. In 1923 she travelled to New York City to study design and decoration before embarking on a fifteen-month European tour, during which she met and married the painter and sculptor Meyer Wolfe.

From 1929 to 1933 she continued to take photographs both in San Francisco, where she became friends with Edward Weston and Dorothea Lange, and in the mountains of Tennessee during the years of the depression. In 1933 her first published photograph appeared in the magazine *Vanity Fair*. From 1936 to 1958 she worked for Carmel Snow, the editor of *Harper's Bazaar*, photographing fashion, still-life and portraits. During this time she also made many trips abroad. In 1937 her photographs were included in the first photographic exhibition at the Museum of Modern Art in New York when she exhibited with Steichen, Stieglitz and Strand. A photograph from this show was published in the *New York Herald Tribune*. It was the first picture of a black person ever to appear in that newspaper.

In 1961 she effectively retired and now lives in New Jersey, where she is working on a book of her own photographs. Her work is on show in the San Francisco Museum of Modern Art, the Gibbs Art Gallery, Charleston, North Carolina, and the Museum of Modern Art, New York. Louise Dahl-Wolfe has played a vital role in the development of fashion photography and many of today's great fashion photographers, such as Penn and Avedon, owe much to her pioneering vision.

'Photography is not fine art. It is an amalgam of individual taste grafted on to mechanical proficiency.'

What made you become a photographer?

I was attending the San Francisco Institute of Art and I was intent on becoming a painter. I began by painting in oils and the teacher said that my work had the richness and quality of a Vermeer! I became very big-headed. One day I decided to change my style and to work with a palette-knife rather than a brush. The teacher who had praised me said my new work was the essence of superficiality. I was so hurt and shocked that my painting career came to an end: I became a photographer in the embryonic stage of existence.

When I was in San Francisco I wanted to be the world's greatest still-life painter. Later when I took up photography I was influenced by the writer Clive Bell, who, together with Roger Fry, was very interested in the aesthetics of shape and form. I shot this photograph of apples on a plate against a black oil cloth. The back light was from a window. Of course the apples and the cloth were so close in value that when I printed it I spent hours in the dark-room dodging – covering part of the print being exposed in an attempt to hold back the tone of the oil cloth and to make the form of the apples stand out.

Frank Crowninshield liked this photograph very much and insisted on showing it to Dr Agha at *Vogue*. He immediately pointed his finger at the weakness of my apples. I was very embarrassed. I knew the weakness was there – I just couldn't control it. After that experience I decided I would go to *Harper's*, where I was lucky enough to work continuously with Diana Vreeland, who was the magazine's fashion editor at the time.

Apples on a Plate,
New York, 1915.

One of your very first photographs was published in Vanity Fair. *Can you tell me about it?*

Vanity Fair was a marvellous magazine. All the great European artists worked for it. It was just about the only cultural magazine in existence. Steichen was the photographer there. He was the man who did most for modern photography and the young people would flock to his lectures because he was such a great speaker. Everybody wanted to work for *Vanity Fair* and it was my ambition too.

This was the first picture that I ever took with my 7×5 camera and at the same time I fulfilled my ambition to work for *Vanity Fair* because they published it. It was of a neighbour of ours. We were living in the Tennessee mountains at the time, in the heart of the bootleg liquor territory. They were the most amazing people – quite happy to shoot the Government Revenue men when they came to threaten their livelihood. We had no electricity in the hills and we lived in a log cabin lit by kerosene lamps. Michael, my husband, hitched a line to the car battery which gave me enough power for a red light. You didn't need a green light then because you didn't use colour-corrected film. My next-door neighbour sat for me. After the picture had appeared in *Vanity Fair* it became very famous. It was before Margaret Bourke-White published her photographs of the South. She insisted on wearing her twenty-five year-old hat. She wouldn't take it off, she was so proud of it. The editor of *Vanity Fair* at the time was Frank Crownin-shield. He fell in love with this picture and it became a sensation. Nobody had ever seen a photograph like it.

That was the beginning of my career as a professional photographer. Michael and I had got married in the 1920s and when the depression began we decided to travel across America. We reached the Tennessee hills and stayed there.

What camera had you used before the 7×5?

I bought one in Germany which I still have, although I don't know what it's called. It didn't have a name on it, but I remember it cost me $10. It was around 1919 and everybody else had a Box Brownie. This German camera was like a Brownie but smaller and it was made of wood. It took pocket film of about $2 \times 1\frac{1}{4}$ inches and it had a Graflex so you could actually see what you were photographing. That made an enormous difference. I enjoyed that $10 camera more than any other I've ever owned. I really caught the photography bug at an artists' colony in Tunisia, which is where I first met my husband. The boys would go out and paint all day and I would go out and take photographs.

It was about 1915 or perhaps earlier that I had bought my very first camera. There were no camera shops then, but luckily the man at the local drug store took a real interest in me and sold me a small Eastman with ground glass on the back. It was $3\frac{1}{4} \times 2\frac{1}{4}$, and the film was very slow then and not colour-corrected. You had to put brown panchromatic make-up on your subject's lips to show them up, otherwise red came out as white. Film directors also had to do that to get the right black-and-white value. You used a film pack that looked rather like today's Polaroid pack. The man at the drug store taught me how to gauge the light on my ground glass – it was long before the days of exposure meters, of course.

Then I wanted an enlarger, but he said, 'There's no use in you spending money on an enlarger. I'll tell you how to make one from an apple box and a tin can.' After I'd done this I took the back off my camera and used the camera and lens for focussing. Then I pushed all the clothes out of my closet and set to work with my enlarger. I didn't know anything about temperature, so the prints were rather naïve though they were interesting.

I did the developing in my mother's dishes which infuriated her as she thought I was going to poison the entire family with my chemicals! One day I couldn't seem to get anything out of my print, so I had the brilliant idea of putting it on top of the stove in the kitchen to warm it up. My mother nearly died when she saw me cooking my print on the gas stove!

When I began to progress I bought myself an English camera, a Thornton Pickard. That was my first really good camera. It was a $4\frac{1}{4} \times 3\frac{1}{4}$.

Have you ever used 35mm?

No. I can't stand 35mm cameras. I don't like their proportions – it's such a narrow shape for the length of film. I think 10×8 is a lovely proportion. I particularly like using a Rolleiflex. I would mark my Rolleiflex off on each side to make the picture rectangular and in the proportion I wanted. I crop, too, but I like to compose the picture to the given shape at the time of shooting.

How did you get into fashion photography?

When I was twenty-five I moved to New York and started working for Hearst Publications. I lived at the Three Arts Club and had a fantastic time with all the artists, musicians and painters. Then when I was twenty-eight I went to Paris with a friend of mine. She was a sketcher for *Women's Wear Daily*. We went to all the fashion houses and I fell in love with the Dior and Givenchy creations. Back in New York I had another friend who was working for Bendels. I asked her to lend me some of the store's models and some clothes so I could experiment. The models had been there since the store had opened, so you can imagine what they looked like all those years later! It was probably the best training I could have had – trying to make those forty-year-old models look attractive!

What do you think about today's fashion photographers?

When I see fashion pictures today I get so mad. It's as if the photographer has forgotten what the female form looks like. The models today look like men. They seem to have no grace, no rhythm. The modern photographer no longer notices the natural lines and curves of a woman's body. Women do things differently from men, even when they're trying to copy them. The poses are essentially different. I try to capture that feminine quality.

One of the problems is that today's unfortunate photographers don't really have anything to photograph. Clothes today are so badly made. Instead of flowing away from the model's body, they seem to stand up on their own like pieces of cardboard. When I look at a photograph I can actually tell whether or not the clothes have been well made. A good garment photographs well. It fits the body and has a special, entirely distinctive 'look'. Designers like Dior and Chanel were meticulous. Their clothes were as beautiful on the inside as on the outside.

Do you think Avedon has been influenced by your work?

I know him very well. I would say he was at first, but I think his work has never been as good since he threw away his Rolleiflex. He should have stuck with that camera. His 10×8 work reminds me of passport photographs.

Untitled, California, 1947.

How would you describe your own attitude to photography?

I think I'm a traditionalist. I'm certainly not a great innovator, although I approve of experimenting and using different cameras. Ultimately, photography's a skill you learn like any other – like cooking, for instance. You can't get away from the fact that the camera is fundamentally mechanical. You are dealing with a box. When you've acquired the skill, you then have to apply it with good taste. Good taste is something intrinsic, inherent – you either have it or you don't. It all boils down to that.

Photography is not fine art. It's an amalgam of individual taste grafted on to mechanical proficiency. The camera may be a third eye but it has its limitations – you realize that when you've had formal training in drawing and painting. I envy the freedom my husband has with his beautiful drawings.

Diana Vreeland is a good example of someone with instinctive taste. I was once asked to photograph a ghastly coat and I didn't see how I could make it look good. In a couple of seconds Diana had dressed it up with a cossack hat and wound a few scarves around the model's neck. It was a transformation. The coat looked wonderful. You can't *learn* style like that.

There were very few professional models in the 1930s. How did you manage?

I hated the popular look of the models in the early days. I called it the 'Candy Box' look – it was all translucent white skin, blonde hair and blue eyes. The men loved it, of course. What I liked was yellowish skin and green eyes, and I found it eventually with Betty Bacall and above all with Mary Jane Russell, who was marvellous. This is a photograph of her in a polka dot dress.

Not everyone shared my preferences, of course. I remember the art director of *Harper's*, Brodovich, really hated one picture I took of Betty Bacall. He said it looked as if she'd given her last pint of blood! But there must have been something good about it because after that she was asked to go to Hollywood, and subsequently – as Lauren Bacall – she signed a contract with a big studio.

What did you look for in your prints?

I always tried to get the values right. I was never very good at getting the exposures right and I had trouble reading the meters, but I was mad about dark-room work. I would have to dodge like mad. I like working in the dark-room because I know what I want from a picture and I know how to get it by manipulating the print. I never understand how today's young photographers can hand their work over to a photographic laboratory. You have no control if you do that. The whole industry now seems to be 'instant' – instant cameras, instant film, instant rush. In my day a photographer had to know every aspect of the craft. Printing and developing has to be a part of it. I love the variety and the different kind of mood that you can extract from one image.

The trouble is that I'm eighty-seven now. Michael and I don't have much more time together, so I don't like to spend it in the dark-room. When I print, I sometimes spend up to nine hours at a stretch in the dark-room. I get obsessed with it.

What do you feel about photographs selling for very high prices and becoming collector's items?

I don't mind people collecting anything, but if they think they're collecting fine art by collecting photography, they're wrong. Actually when you take inflation into account the price of photographs hasn't risen all that much.

Untitled, Paris, 1952.

Louise Dahl-Wolfe

Untitled, California, 1947.

You are famous for your photographs of nudes. How do they relate to your fashion photography?

Working in a life class at the San Francisco Institute helped me a lot with my later fashion photographs. I drew from the nude, so when I began to photograph women who were dressed I knew exactly how their clothes should hang to enhance the model's figure. The nude has been very important to me. It was seeing Anne Brigman's nudes in her Oakland studio that first made me interested in photography. I saw the possibilities.

What sort of lighting did you use?

Initially I used a series of Mazda lights. Later I bought theatre lights. I would use one over the model's head. Then I had another 5000 watt spotlight that would light the whole side – like the sun coming in through a window.

Let's talk for a moment about one or two of your contemporaries. What are your memories of Steichen?

He was a nice, warm human being. I remember going to one of his lectures when he said that, before the days of exposure meters, he was the best guesser in the business. Then one day the Weston people gave him a light meter and he used it on a shot of

Washington Bridge. He admitted it had out-guessed him. God knows where photography would be today without him. I was offered a contract by *Vanity Fair*, for whom he worked, but they stipulated I had to work from the National Magazine studio. I was too much of a free spirit for that, so I turned it down.

Who else have you admired?

George Hoyningen-Huene was a very good friend and a marvellous photographer, especially in his earlier work. Avedon, of course. At his exhibition at MOMA he paid me a great compliment, saying, in front of all the photographers and prominent people in the art world, 'There's Louise Dahl-Wolfe. Make way. I go to her – she doesn't come to me.' I was rather embarrassed!

Louise Dahl-Wolfe

Untitled, Jamaica.

Robert Doisneau

Robert Doisneau was born in 1912 in the Paris suburb of Gentilly. In 1926, encouraged by his parents, he went to the Ecole Estienne where he studied engraving, recèiving his diploma in 1929. From the age of fourteen, however, he had been interested in photography. He did some advertising photography on leaving the engraving school and in 1931 went to work for the sculptor André Vigneau as a photographer. He mastered the techniques of the medium during this period, taking both architectural and fashion pictures. At weekends he would take to the streets of Paris with an old, wooden 10 × 8 camera and tripod, capturing the magical moments of sweet humour for which he has become famous. In 1932 his first story, 'The Flea Market', was sold to *Excelsior* magazine.

From 1934 to 1939 he worked at the Renault car company at Billancourt on the outskirts of Paris as an industrial photographer, a job he did not enjoy. In the evenings he would work in his laboratory perfecting a colour printing process he had invented. Luckily he was fired by Renault for being consistently late. In 1939 he met Charles Rado, founder of Agence Rapho, which represented Brassaï among others. It was the start of a lifelong relationship with the agency.

At the outbreak of war Doisneau joined the infantry, but illness led to his return to Paris where he spent the war years. His engraving skills were used to forge documents for the French Resistance. He continued to take reportage pictures, illustrated a book on French science and made postcards for the Army Museum.

In 1945 he briefly joined the Alliance Photo press agency but in the following year he rejoined the reopened Rapho agency. In 1950 and 1951 he worked for *Vogue* magazine, for financial reasons, taking fashion photographs. After that he worked regularly for a variety of magazines, especially *Life* and *Picture Post*. In 1947 he was awarded the Prix Kodak and in 1956 the Prix Niépce. In 1973 he made a short film called *Le Paris de Robert Doisneau*. Today he still lives and works in Paris.

Doisneau has constantly returned to, and gained his inspiration from, the streets of his native Paris. Like Kertész, Atget and Brassaï, he developed an eye for the rare moment in the commonplace event, a phenomenon often invisible to a less creative vision. But Doisneau, perhaps more than any other photographer in the history of the medium, grafted on to his reportage photographs a beautiful humour that unfailingly brings a smile to the face of the beholder. There is about the pictures of this remarkable artist a quintessential *joie de vivre*, a celebration of the lighter side of life, that is no less evident in his delightful personality. As yet his international reputation, although formidable, has perhaps not adequately reflected his massive contribution to photography. In coming years this state of affairs is sure to be remedied.

His one-man exhibitions include shows at the Museum of Modern Art, Chicago, in 1960; the Bibliothèque Nationale, Paris, in 1968; the George Eastman House, Rochester, New York, in 1972; the Witkin Gallery, New York in 1978; and the Musée d'Art Moderne, Paris, in 1979.

———•———

When did your interest in photography begin?

When I was about fourteen. I had always looked at the people around me with a critical eye and wanted to capture them. At first I started to draw them, but the moment was soon gone and I had to draw from memory. So my thoughts started to turn to photography. Actually I was too shy to confront people face to face so I intended to use photography to record the environment rather than people. I started off in an engraving school. I never wanted to be an engraver, but my parents chose it for me as a profession, thinking that it would be a good, steady job.

In those days photographers were rather looked down on. My family thought it would be a terrible profession to be in, always hanging around on street corners with layabouts! My aunt, whom the family considered to be rather posh, would introduce me as an engraver, never a photographer, long after I had given up engraving.

In 1934 I got a job as an industrial photographer with the Renault car company. I worked there for five years although I never really liked the job. I had to take pictures of all the machinery – lathes and milling machines. The only way I could do it was with a 24 × 18 camera and the equipment used to weigh about 20kg.

I used to dream a lot of my time away, hoping that someone would come up to me and say, 'Robert, there's a man in the other room waiting for you.' And when I saw this man he'd say, 'Doisneau, I've heard all about your colour prints. They're supposed to be magnificent. I have my car outside. Come with me. I must see them immediately.' You see, I'd been experimenting with colour printing. It was my escape from factory life. I'd perfected a printing process which I'd work away at every night in my kitchen.

Can you talk about that process?

I don't see why not. I can't imagine that Kodak will steal my secret formula now! I'd make a tricolour separation of a subject and with the negative that I made I would isolate three gelatins previously tinted with primary colours and filled with bichromate. Then I'd peel off the gelatins in a warm mix of disinfectant and wood shavings before transferring them on to celluloid polished with paraffin and beeswax. I would then transfer the three pictures on to my final background and place them, very carefully, in order – yellow, red and then blue – making sure that they were perfectly lined up. The result gave a rather naïve version of how I imagine people with bad eyesight see the world!

Well, I thought my discovery would change everything – or at least it might secure my release from industrial photography. But life isn't like that. Shattering innovations that change the course of one's history don't often happen. What changed me was a man from the manager's office. He sacked me for being late!

I was really excited to be back on the streets. So during the Second World War I became a photojournalist, taking photographs of people in the streets and bars of Paris.

Were you influenced by any painters?

Yes, bad painters! Not Picasso, not modern artists. I was very influenced by a painting of Lady Godiva – well, perhaps more by the subject matter than the actual painting! I remember the light was very theatrical and I liked that a lot then.

What made you take up photography rather than painting?

Well, when at last I rid myself of the etching studio I thought, 'Now I'll do exactly what artists have been doing for years.' You see, they've always been obsessed with ideas of accuracy. I thought that if I was going to imitate, then I might as well do it more accurately than any painter could – so I turned to the camera. I captured images as conscientiously as I could and that's what I still do. Sometimes I think I 'see' more than other people. When I feel that, it's a comfort – but the feeling only comes from time to time.

When did you lose your shyness?

When I found I could hide behind my Rolleiflex. It was even better with the plate camera because I could put this black curtain over my head and I didn't have to look at people directly. I use both a Nikon and a Pentax now, but I think they're very aggressive cameras. With the Rolleiflex you seem to salute people. I'd use it all the time even today, but you only have one lens. In fact the Nikon 35mm has been a blessing to reportage photographers.

When I first started to take photos I'd put this great wooden 10×8 camera down on the pavement, screw it into the tripod, pull the black cloth over my head and feel totally secure in the knowledge that no one could see me. Of course it didn't make me invisible – I just *felt* inconspicuous. One day when I'd finished focussing I came up for a breath of fresh air and there were all these characters standing around and staring at me. Not a good feeling for a shy man. One of them called me a fool. It wasn't a very good start to photography. Anyway despite that my determination was rock-hard – like cement – and most Sundays I could be found at the flea market in Paris beneath my black cloth. The results, I'm glad to say, were published by *Excelsior* magazine.

As a shy man do you worry about the privacy of your subjects? Do you ask their permission before you photograph them?

No, but afterwards I write to them. I have long exchanges of letters. Last Sunday for instance I wrote fourteen such letters. After I've taken the photograph I ask them for their address and we talk. I'm very friendly with people. I like them very much.

Have you done any commercial work?

Yes, I've done many things for advertising. I don't like to, because it restricts my freedom. What I like is to roam around Paris all day long, to be free to walk. That's the most important thing for me.

Do you shoot much film?

It's very irregular. In the last four months I've shot twenty rolls of film – that's all. I work a lot in my lab, printing. I love to print, but then I don't have time to shoot.

Coco, Paris, 1952

Can we talk about this selection of photographs? Let's start with this one of the man in a bowler hat.

This picture is called *Coco*. I shot it in a bistro in La Belle Etoile in 1952. I used to go there almost every night, so that the people would get to know me. They were real down-and-outs. This man had been a soldier in the Foreign Legion. He would usually have a stuffed parrot with him whose name was Coco, so everybody called this man after his parrot. Coco used to think he was still a soldier and he'd play the drum on the table, just like a soldier.

I shot that particular picture on a Rolleiflex.

Didn't you ever feel scared among such low-life company?

It was a strange world in that café, but a friend of mine knew it well so it wasn't dangerous for me to go there.

And what about the muscle-man – was he one of them?

The man lying on the bed was a docker, but in the evenings he'd work in the streets and in cabaret making a little money by sticking pins in his arms. He was 'The Insensible Man'. I met him in a café. I hadn't known him for long – only four or five days – and he invited me back to his room because he thought I might be interested in the drawings on his wall that he thought were photographs. As soon as I saw them they reminded me of long-distance lorry drivers' pin-ups, so I asked him to lie on the bed and I took this photograph. He became very possessive about me and when he introduced me to his friends he'd say, 'This is Robert, my personal photographer.' Alas, I lost touch with him. This picture is the parody of the masculine man.

Pinups, Paris, 1952.

Robert Doisneau

Respectful Homage, Paris,
1952.

This one is called *Respectful Homage*. There was a theatre in Montmartre, the Concert Maillol, and I would go to the matinée performances. The same people would sit in the first five rows day after day. Each day one chosen client would be invited to sit backstage and watch the show from the wings.

Robert Doisneau

Tell me about Picasso and the Loaves.

This picture of Picasso was a pleasure to take. When I arrived at Villauris Picasso was having lunch with his wife and we talked, but we didn't shoot any pictures. I came back the next day having realized by then that Picasso had a great sense of the ridiculous. I went to a baker I knew, who made the bread rolls that are on the table. The baker used to call them Picasso's hands. When people pointed out that they had only four fingers he'd say, 'Of course, that's why they're called Picasso's hands.' So I bought the rolls and put them in front of Picasso and took the photograph. You know he loved to make jokes – we spent two days joking all the time. Picasso was the best model I ever had. Everyone coming close to him received some gold dust.

Picasso and the Loaves,
Villauris, 1952.

Brothers, Paris, c. 1932.

And Brothers? *Was that difficult to shoot?*

This is an old picture that I shot around 1932, when I first started to do reportage. I mainly photographed children because I felt very shy with adults. Children on the other hand thought it was fun to have their pictures taken. I waited for a few hours to get this picture. The two boys in the foreground, walking on their hands, were further up the road at first but I felt sure that they wouldn't be able to resist the temptation to show off in front of the other two boys. Sure enough they did just that. Actually it was rather easy to get this picture. All I needed was patience.

This picture known as Sidelong Glance *is one of your best-known photographs. How did you get it?*

In order to take this picture of the couple looking through the window I hid the Rolleiflex in an old chair. It was very carefully concealed. I just waited for people to come by and photographed their reactions. At the time, that painting was considered to be in very bad taste – very crude. I shot the sequence of pictures for *Life* magazine.

Sidelong Glance, Paris, 1948.

Elliott Erwitt

Elliot Erwitt was born in Paris in 1928, the son of Russian émigré parents. At high school in Hollywood he became interested in photography and worked part time as a printer and processor for a company providing publicity prints for the Hollywood film studios. When he was sixteen he bought an old plate camera and started to experiment. At that stage photography seemed to him to be 'a reasonable way of making a living'.

'All the technique in the world doesn't compensate for the inability to notice.'

In 1948, after attending classes at the Los Angeles City College, he moved to New York where his first job was to take pictures of famous authors for book jackets. He worked mainly with authors from the Knopf publishing house and during this period photographed, among others, H. L. Mencken, Thomas Mann and Conrad Richter.

Edward Steichen saw and admired his work and got him a job at the studio of Valentino Sarra, a commercial photographer. Later Erwitt worked with Roy Stryker, the former head of the Farm Security Administration Historical Division, and travelled with him to Pittsburgh to document the city for the Mellon Foundation.

In 1951 he joined the army where he worked as a dark-room technician. While stationed in France he visited the Paris offices of Magnum where he met Robert Capa, who suggested that, on leaving the army, he should join the organization. This he did in 1953. Erwitt became President of Magnum in 1959 and campaigned actively for photographers' rights.

Since then he has worked in films, advertising, photojournalism and architectural photography, and his work has been published in most of the world's magazines. His work is part of the permanent collections at the Museum of Modern Art, New York; the Smithsonian Institution; the Bibliothèque Nationale, Paris; and numerous other museums and galleries around the world.

Elliott Erwitt is a humorous man with a finely developed sense of the comic and the ridiculous. His personal photographs rely on keenly observed juxtapositions. They poke gentle fun at the world in a kind and economical way, deflating pomposity, exposing hypocrisy. He is a bitter enemy of pretension in photography and hates wordy explanations and pseudo-intellectual comments on his photographs, which he firmly believes should be allowed to speak for themselves. He has no time for artistic posturings which scorn the commercial aspects of photography. His commissioned work and his own personal photographs are complementary – the one gives him the freedom to produce the other. In a medium that is sometimes in danger of too great a preoccupation with its own mysteries and techniques, Elliott Erwitt's brilliantly witty work is a refreshing reminder that life is fun and that photography, as part of life, is no exception.

———•———

Have you been influenced by any particular photographer?

No, but all the great photographers have influenced me to some extent – people like Cartier-Bresson, Atget and Kertész. Steichen helped me a bit when he was in charge of the Department of Photography at MOMA. He actually arranged a job for me with Valentino Sarra when I needed one. He also bought a number of my pictures for the permanent collection at MOMA. He has encouraged a lot of other photographers, too, in that way.

Do you mix much with other photographers?

No, although I do have a few friends from Magnum. Groups of photographers are like gatherings of dentists or psychiatrists – they get together and talk shop. I find that I'm interested in my subjects, not in my colleagues. Travelling and pointing my camera at people is what I like to do.

I've just been talking to Doisneau. What do you think of him?

Doisneau is a wonderful photographer. He has a very unusual way of putting things. He's highly intelligent and he's also literate, which is rare for a photographer. I think he's finally getting the attention he deserves. The reason he has not attracted a lot of notice before is that he's not a good public relations man – and that's all part of his charm.

Magnum has been important in your life and through it you've fought and won many battles for photographers. Tell me about the organization.

Magnum is a co-operative and I'm one of the owners. It's a group to which all the members contribute a percentage of their earnings. I've been represented by and associated with Magnum since I came out of the army in 1953. Through Magnum I fought for the rights of photographers to own their own negatives – to do whatever they wished with them. Magnum has had an important influence on the way photography is regarded, but it hasn't had any influence on my own work.

One of your books used the words 'Anti-Photograph' in the title. Why was that?

It was just a catchy title. The man who thought it up once told me why it was appropriate, but I've totally forgotten what he said! In general I'm against titles for books and photographs. I describe my photos with a place and a date. The picture speaks better than words.

What do you think about fashion photography?

It's the simplest-minded photography of all. I loathe the mystique that surrounds it – all those silly people taking silly pictures. The most necessary attribute of a fashion photographer is to be an excellent salesman. He is essentially taking identification photographs of women who've been carefully prepared by great designers, hairdressers and the finest make-up artists. Then the fashion photographer comes along with his wind machines and motor drives and records the models. They're not doing much, but they have to pretend they are. It's quite enterprising in a way. I'm not against people making a living by taking fashion pictures – or passport photographs – but I'm against the pretension that goes with it, although from a marketing viewpoint I suppose it's necessary. Without all that mystique they probably wouldn't earn anything!

Do you think there have been any great fashion photographers?

I suppose out of the thousands there are half a dozen that stand out from the crowd. Avedon was interesting at the beginning of his career. He was one of the innovators, but who cares about innovation in fashion photography? I've been on the fringes of it, and I guess it's amusing for a couple of weeks. But imagine devoting your life to it! When somebody does do something inventive, it's repeated until everyone is bored. You know – someone uses a little Vaseline on the lens and that's repeated for ages. Then somebody else decides it would be fun to kick the camera stand, and you see that for a bit. I'm oversimplifying, but you get the idea.

At Elliott Erwitt's request, all his photographs are uncaptioned.

93

Elliott Erwitt

John Szarkowski once said that your pictures dealt with the empty spaces between happenings. He has used the phrase 'The Indecisive Moment' to describe the subject matter of your photos. What do you think of that?

I had heard about 'The Indecisive Moment', but not the empty spaces. Did he really say that? It sounds good, doesn't it? Sounds deep!

So you find remarks like that about your work a bit pretentious – what do you feel about pretensions?

I like them – in my subjects! I'm very much against intellectualizing and 'clever' rationalizations of the reasons and motives behind one's work. The picture is the important thing. I always want to replace the words in photographic books with pictures. If there must be words, they should be left to the professional writers. The problem is it's difficult to get publishers interested in what a picture book should be. They like structures and themes because that's what the book market wants. Publishers say that to sell a book you need pictures of naked girls, or landscapes or seascapes, or sunsets or close-ups of flowers. That way you appeal to an 'identifiable' market.

Actually it's quite surprising that the books I've produced have been published at all because they're really monographs, collections of the snaps I've taken. They're a response to what I see. One of those books was actually sold as a 'dog' book – which it wasn't – because the editors had identified a market that liked dogs. The books that I want to do would just be selections of photographs taken at random, with little or no accompanying text and no structure.

You earn your living from your advertising photography, but it's the photographs you take for personal reasons that seem to me the most interesting.

When you're doing a job for a client and getting paid for it it's quite a different matter from taking pictures for your own amusement. When you're working for others there are rules and briefs that have to be fulfilled. You only have freedom when you're working for yourself. Of course the personal work often leads to commercial jobs, and the commissioned work also allows me to take my own photographs. The two situations are just different – sometimes I choose one, sometimes the other. The flexibility lets me live in a manner and style that satisfies me. The personal work is a bonus and gives me great pleasure.

What in your view are the most important qualities a good photographer needs?

Anyone can become a photographer by buying a camera, just as anyone can become a writer by buying a pencil, but to be good requires more than mere technical skill. You can tell immediately if someone is good. They're gifted with a sense of style, a sense of composition and a sense of sense. It's instinctive. All the technique in the world doesn't compensate for the inability to notice things. In fact it just gets in the way. The most important thing is to be able to 'see'.

Nevertheless, how important to you is technique?

The content is the most important thing. If the content is there, controlling what happens to the print is no problem. For me, printing is of secondary concern. The vital

part is the actual taking of the picture. To some extent that's intuitive – you don't think too hard about it beforehand. It happens very quickly.

Which lens do you prefer to work with?

That's a difficult question to answer. I use whatever lens is appropriate, but when I carry a camera around for pleasure I have a lighter lens on, so I suppose a lot of my work gets shot on a 50mm lens.

What do you feel about collecting photography? Do you own the prints of other photographers?

Yes I have a few. Josef Koudelka, Kertész, and other colleagues of mine at Magnum. I like almost all of their fine pictures.

What are you doing in London at the moment?

I'm making part of a documentary film on luxury that I'm shooting around the world. It's an amusing look at the pursuit of expensive pleasure. On Saturday, for instance, I'm doing a Harley Street doctor who rejuvenates you with special injections. The film is commissioned by Home Box Office, an American cable television company owned by Time Inc. I did an hour-long documentary for them last year on the modelling profession and it did well, so I've got a large budget this time. I find making movies challenging, though it's almost impossible to stay inside the budget no matter how big it is to start with.

What do you feel is the relationship between moving pictures and stills?

I don't think really there is one, except that both are visual.

Comedy and a keen sense of the ridiculous are obviously important in your work.

I once wanted to be a clown and I once wanted to be a comedy writer. Also I'm attracted to emotional situations, and I'm bored by serious people.

Ralph Gibson

Ralph Gibson is a conceptualist, fascinated by the theory and philosophy of photography, whose frontiers he is continually striving to extend. He lives and works in New York City, and is also a successful publisher of photographic books. Born in Los Angeles in 1939, he grew up in Hollywood and in 1956 joined the United States Navy, where he studied photography. In 1960 he went to the San Francisco Art Institute, after which he became assistant to Dorothea Lange in 1962. In 1966 he moved to New York where he worked with Robert Frank, and in the same year his book *The Strip* was published. A second book, *The Hawk*, appeared two years later. In 1969 Gibson founded his own publishing company, Lustrum Press, under whose imprint appeared his next three photographic books, *The Somnambulist*, *Déjà-Vu*, and *Days at Sea*. (Details of these and other books by Gibson are given in the Bibliography.) In 1973 and 1976 he received grants from the National Endowment for the Arts.

Gibon's work is exhibited in over twenty-five public collections including those of the Museum of Modern Art and the Metropolitan Museum of Art in New York; the National Gallery of Canada; the Bibliothèque Nationale, Paris; the Pasadena Museum of Art; the International Museum of Photography in Rochester, New York; and the Center for Creative Photography, University of Arizona, Tucson. He has had over forty one-man exhibitions and has taken part in as many group shows. The former include exhibitions at the San Francisco Art Institute; the Pasadena Museum of Art; the Palais des Beaux-Arts, Brussels; the Leo Castelli Gallery, New York; the Baltimore Museum of Art; the Swedish Museum of Photography, Stockholm; the Museum of Modern Art, Oxford; the Galerie Fiolet, Amsterdam; and the University of Guelph, Canada.

'I'm not interested in anything except filling the surface of my print with the high tension of a snare drum.'

101

What is your chief interest in photography now?

Ever since I stopped working as a documentary photographer around 1967 I have been trying to get as far from the documentary approach as possible and instead to work in an extremely personal way. The truths that I wanted to locate and to isolate were deep within me and had very little to do with society, or the role of the media in society. Interestingly enough, the relaxation of this documentary restriction opened up enormous possibilities for me.

Around 1968, when I started work on my first book, *The Somnambulist*, I wanted to get from one place to the next and modulate and so I made that sequence of forty-eight pictures. I was quite satisfied with it – it had its moments.

However, it wasn't until 1972 when I published *Déjà-Vu*, containing the spread of the hand with the gun and the boy on the pier, that I felt I had actually located the idea for which I had been searching for some time.

Can you explain that idea?

To understand the concept you have to know something about music. There is a theory that if you take a guitar and hit a C chord, of which the notes are CEC, then while those three notes are resonating they combine to produce additional tonalities which cannot be reached directly. This is called a sonic overtone. People like Stravinsky, who composed cacophonous, structured music, are actually reaching for those overtones. In my photographs I'm striving for a similar effect, which I call 'visual overtones'.

How does that work in practice – for instance in relation to the picture of the hand gun and the one of the boy on the pier?

I shot the picture of the hand with the gun in Santa Fe, New Mexico. I was with my friend Larry Clark, and we were out playing with a .22 Magnum. The idea was that the cartridge would fire the bullet in a straight line into space. I had a sort of conceptual 'hit'. It occurred to me that as soon as the bullet went off, even before you could register the sound, it would be far across the horizon, in a straight, then slowly curving, arcing, descending line. I had taken the companion picture of the man on the pier in New York City six months before.

The moment I saw those two pictures side by side I knew that the problem was how to leap the gutter from one to the other in a way that would create distance within the grey matter of the viewer. It's an example of *déjà-vu*. When you have such an experience it fades so fast that you lose the memory of it in seconds. My theory was that the man in New York City would raise his hand, the gesture would be completed three thousand miles away in New Mexico, and the bullet would go off a fraction of a second later. After all, that's still about a thousand times slower than the average telecommunications laser beam travels.

Did lighting play a significant part in achieving the paired effect here?

Generally I insist that the lighting value remains constant, but despite the fact that in the picture of the man with black hair the sky is somewhat overcast, the *tonality* matches up with the vivid blue sky of New Mexico. Notice how in the picture of the man there's a shadow in the lower left-hand part of the frame at the side of his left arm. That shadow relates very effectively to the shadow beneath the forearm in the fist holding the gun. That's a distinct subliminal connection. I know that people don't stop to analyze those things, but I am utterly convinced of the fact that we do perceive subliminally, instantaneously – and that we respond to that perception.

Tell me more about the pairing of photographs.

Usually they have to match exactly in terms of scale, distance of subject matter, proportion, and size of the two prints to be juxtaposed. These are primary concerns. When I worked on *The Somnambulist* I made all the pictures the same size, but then I noticed that the right-hand page captured all one's attention. So I thought that I would experiment in *Déjà-Vu* by making the right-hand prints small and the left-hand ones large. This meant that I had to make all the prints in two sizes, as I didn't know at that stage which page each picture was going to go on.

In the 'hand with the gun' spread I had originally intended to put the larger picture on the left, but in the end I put it on the right because it worked better that way. This has a bearing on my 'point of departure' theory.

And what is that theory?

Years ago, when I had been working for Dorothea Lange for about a year, I eventually got round to showing her my prints, and she said, 'Oh, Ralph, I see your problem. You have no point of departure.' She said that if you go down to the drug store to buy toothpaste you have a much greater chance of finding something significant than if you just stand on a street corner waiting for it to happen. For five years after that I was effectively standing on a street corner. Only when I started working on *The Somnambulist* did I realize that 'point of departure' was a wonderful theory. I started out by saying, 'I'm going to put the smaller picture on the right-hand page and the large one on the left,' and that was the 'point of departure' that led me to the possibility of reversing that order. The important thing is to have an objective. You try something and it could be terrible in itself, but it might lead you to something a little better.

Has the concept of pairing led you on to anything else?

Pairing has been important, and I have begun to realize that the most characteristic, intrinsic thing about my vision and my voice – the thing that is most 'me' – is not necessarily my feelings for surrealism, as many people have thought. My real interest is in syntax. In fact I'm working now on a book called *Syntax*, in which the entire point is going to be how pictures work à propos of one another.

Western civilization shows an exceptionally high degree of visual sophistication evidenced by, and perhaps also the result of, the high quality of our media – publishing, cinema and, most of all, television. So perhaps my little theories of 'visual overtones' are small fry. However my theories of syntax probably *are* interesting in the context of where *photography* is today, as opposed to other methods of non-verbal communication.

How do you define photography's relationship with reality?

In 1975 I was working on a series entitled *Quadrants* in which all the pictures were made at three feet; one of them was the photograph of the priest. It remains one of my most personally satisfying images because it has everything I want à propos of photography and of photography's relation to reality and of my relationship to both reality and photography. That is to say that formally it is very clean; the proportions are there; there are big areas of black; it has a little geometry; and it maintains a fixed view of reality. The close-up attachment on my Leica that enabled me to take these pictures satisfied my yearning for simplicity. I had been seeking, searching for it since the beginning. I'm not interested in anything except filling the surface of my print with the high tension of a snare drum. I want to empty out anything that is superfluous. I'm not

Overleaf left and right: Untitled, Santa Fe, New Mexico, *c.* 1972.

interested in providing vast textural information. There are many reasons why these pictures work or don't work. When I miss I do so by a very slim margin, but an eighth of an inch is as good as a mile.

Can you say something about the other picture in this spread?

This is a nude that I took during a workshop in Arles in 1979. I was interested primarily in the triangulation between her lip, the little armpit, and then this open space on the left. There is an interesting tension between the lower left-hand corner and the lower right-hand corner. Now occasionally, rather than being abstract, I like to get a little corny, and it occurs to me that the priest and the girl are in perfect proportion to one another. One represents sacred, the other profane, love. You can't have a greater dichotomy than a priest in black and a young, white nude. They are diametrically opposed.

In terms of positive and negative I like this spread. It's often difficult to gauge just how graphic one can let the work become. I like the impact of contrasts because it tends to arrest the viewer. It wipes the slate clean in the viewer's conscience and makes him more receptive to the kind of abstract, slightly open-ended or unresolved kind of statement that I like my work to make. I need to have total attention in order to produce this.

Have you used these two pictures in a spread before?

No, although I always knew that I intended to.

Do you like photographing the female form?

I've been photographing nudes from the start. For various reasons I find that the female form will reflect just about any set of formal or visual concerns that I might have. I can get all the shapes that I want from the female body. When your work is in black-and-white, as mine is, you are continually involved in notions of positive and negative – space, forms and shapes. Often the black shapes harbour more content than the white or the middle grey ones.

The next pair is of the same woman on two different, although adjacent, islands. The picture on the right, of the hand with the mirror, was made in Corsica a year earlier than the one with the shadow on her face, which was shot in Sardinia. I consider the latter to be a portrait, at least a portrait in parts, in shapes. It's a kind of Cubist idea, even though the shapes are not very Cubist, except maybe the shadow on her face. Cubism attempts to see things from four sides at once, which opens up the subject. The space between the two pictures harbours just as much content as the pictures themselves.

The one of the hand with the mirror I sometimes playfully call 'The Birth of the Apostrophe', because of the shape of her nostril. I like the shapes, the kind of flowing, curvaceous things that happen in a woman's figure, as for instance the arm with the bracelet. Note that the upper left-hand corner has a slight degree of distortion and is also a little soft in focus, two things I don't normally do. This is simply because I was in very close. I could not have held the depth of field and still produced the same effect. Both pictures were taken with a 50mm lens with the dual-range Silicron.

Overleaf left and right:
Untitled, Arles, 1979.

Ralph Gibson

How do you relate your work to that of other more traditional photographers?

Pairing the photographs is interesting because the sum equals more than the total of the parts. It's a way for me to make more of the medium. I'm not interested in the merely conventional truths of photography – the 'old people, children, dogs' school of photography doesn't satisfy my needs any longer. I did it for a long time and I admire the work of the great photographers, many of whom are my friends.

Take for instance *the* great traditional purist, Cartier-Bresson. He once admitted to me that when he first came out with his pictures in the 1930s they were considered highly radical. The same is true of both Kertész and Lartigue. Cartier-Bresson told me that we owe everything to Kertész, and Kertész told me, 'Yes, I've heard that he says that, and I wish he'd stop!' Anyway, clearly these were the guys who invented photography. Lartigue invented its calligraphy, and Kertész added poetry. Whereas Lartigue confined himself to certain subject matter, Kertész would make a good picture out of just about anything.

It's hard to do anything in photography well, and I know this because I've attempted many different forms of it – I've been at it since I was seventeen. Until 1970 I did fashion, industrial, advertising – anything I could shoot with a 35mm. Fifteen years ago you had to be a documentary photographer and work for *Life* or you were out of it. Even the great master, Brandt, was a documentary photographer until 1950, and then his nudes were so radical that nobody knew what the hell to do with them. Now they are household items, as easy to grasp as anything. Cartier-Bresson's earlier Surrealist works are very easy to understand now. You know, in a way *these* are the 'good old days' of photography. They are happening right now before our eyes.

What are your ambitions?

I'm not the kind of photographer who can be content to perform high variations on previously announced themes. I'm not saying that those who do that are insignificant. What I want to do, however, is to extend the existing definition of the medium, and I only want to take the kind of photographs that will allow me to do that.

A lot of my effort now is centred on the attempt to understand my own creative process. The simple truth is that very little is known about the evolution of a creative photographer. All our great photographers are much older than me and they haven't kept records. I keep journals and write a lot about my work, because I want to understand about my own creative process so that I can develop and produce more significant work as I get older. I think that is why the Center for Creative Photography in Tucson inaugurated an archive for me. They are not usually interested in somebody as young as myself.

I want to produce more, but I seem to average no more than fifteen signable works a year. The fact that time seems to be moving faster gives me the impression that I am producing less. Also the kind of pictures that I want to take now are much more difficult than my previous works, and I reject so much. Sometimes, as my eye changes and my personality modulates, I come to accept pictures that I have rejected earlier. This is the extreme intellectual pleasure of being an artist, that things change pretty consistently for the better.

How do you respond to the images you have created?

I'm interested in making pictures that have philosophical and psychological implications, pictures that provoke. I don't care how the camera sees. I want to make it see the way I see. The truth is that I am becoming increasingly minimal and producing works that have more staying power. I can look at them for longer periods. What do you see in my studio? Photographs. I always live with my work. I must be surrounded by my own images, and maybe a few others, all the time. I want to see them through every aspect of my personality – when I'm asleep, awake, happy, sad, anything. No matter what, my work is speaking to me and eventually I can understand it. The kind of pictures that I take don't always make that easy, and especially for me as the photographer. It means that I have to understand not only the picture but also myself – who, why and what has made this thing. My pictures keep me honest, and I enjoy that.

This seems very much an artist's viewpoint. Would you agree?

Obviously this kind of attitude to the medium totally precludes the possibility of working commercially. I certainly couldn't use this apparatus to flog soap. I *was* a freelance photographer until I was about thirty, and when *The Somnambulist* was published and made it I was able to quit. Then I could sell an occasional interview, give a workshop, have a show, get a grant. The result is that nobody sits in judgement on my work. Nobody calls me up and tells me what to shoot. I decide what to shoot and I judge whether or not it's any good. So now I live primarily from the sale of my prints and from my publishing ventures. I show continually – that's how you get the work out there and sell it. Marcel Duchamp said the artist must do that.

Your books are an important part of your output. Would you like to say something about the relationship between your writing and your photographs?

For me there is always a cognitive moment when something snaps inside my head – then I know the language is being spoken. One doesn't really want to explain one's work, nor tell one's viewers how to perceive it, but years ago I studied with a mystic who told me that one can only fully understand those things that can be spoken about. If you can't speak meaningfully about something, then you don't really understand it. Well, I like to write and speak about my work, and I always find somebody who will read and listen. By doing so I come to understand my work more deeply.

How would you sum up the work you are doing now?

One of the key aspects of my work as it has become minimal is the fact that I don't want to make allegorical, narrative photographs. My pictures don't tell a story, but in their better moments they *do* provoke visual concern.

Some years ago I came to understand that I am not interested in making abstract photographs, but I *am* interested in photographing the abstract in things. This is a decidedly metaphysical approach. Reading things into a photograph is the prerogative of both the artist and the viewer. Often people come to me with work into which they are reading all kinds of schmaltz that just isn't happening. This is one of the pitfalls in taking such a poetic licence towards one's work. When it works everybody calls you a hero, and when you miss you're an asshole.

Horst

Horst P. Horst was born in Germany in 1906 and spent his childhood in a large house near the city of Weimar. Artists from the early Bauhaus were frequent visitors to his home. From them he acquired an interest in art and when he was eighteen he went to study the subject in Hamburg because Gropius was teaching there. In 1925 he moved to Paris, intending to become an architect, and worked for a time with Le Corbusier. Financial reasons prevented him from completing his studies.

In 1931 Horst was given the chance to use the *Vogue* photographic studios in Paris by Dr Agha, an art director, and his first photograph was published by the magazine. He immediately decided on a career in photography and to assist himself spent much time studying art history at the Louvre. In 1932 he had his first photographic exhibition 'in a cellar under an obscure bookshop in Passy'. In 1933 he photographed his first Paris fashion collection.

During the 1930s Horst worked mainly for French *Vogue*. In 1932 he went to New York to work with the legendary Condé Nast, but after a famous row he returned to Paris and immersed himself in the artistic life of the city. Through his close relationship with the designer Coco Chanel he became friendly with many of her famous contemporaries, among them Marcel Duchamp, Salvador Dali, Jean Cocteau, Man Ray, Christian Bérard and Pavel Tchelitchew.

In the early 1930s Horst also became closely associated with the great fashion photographer George Hoyningen-Huene, for whom he worked as a model and occasionally as an assistant. Horst was strongly influenced by the photographic style of his friend and mentor.

In 1939, with the storm clouds of war gathering over Europe, Horst obtained American citizenship and set sail for the USA. He arrived a few days before the outbreak of war. By then the rift with Condé Nast had been healed and from then on Horst was to work regularly for such publications as French, English, Italian and American *Vogue* and *House and Garden*. In New York he was able to renew his collaboration with

I don't think photography has anything remotely to do with the brain. It has to do with eye appeal.'

113

Hoyningen-Huene who had emigrated to America in 1935. On his death in 1968 he left his entire photographic collection to Horst.

During the war Horst served as a sergeant in the Combat Engineers and also worked as a photographer for the US Army magazine, *Yanks*.

Throughout the 1950s and early 1960s he continued to build his reputation as an outstanding fashion photographer. For a period he gave this up to concentrate on photographing interiors, but more recently he has returned once again to the sphere of photography in which his reputation was built.

Horst has had several exhibitions of his work at the Sonnabend Gallery in New York and Paris. He is currently working on his autobiography.

———— • ————

Let's start by discussing this picture of Coco Chanel.

This photograph of Chanel is probably my favourite and it was her favourite portrait of herself. She had had a big row with *Vogue* and they hadn't even been allowed to see her collection for a year or two, let alone take photographs of her and her dresses. She telephoned them one day and said that she wanted to be photographed by me. Of course *Vogue* were madly excited.

Chanel, Paris, 1934.

What was it like to work with her?

She turned up in a white dress and I photographed her in that. It was not a success. She said, 'That's a lovely photograph, but it has nothing to do with me.' I said, 'How can it have anything to do with you? I don't know you.' So she said, 'Come to dinner,' and I did. She made dinner for me and I saw how she lived.

Then she arrived after lunch at the Bois de Boulogne and I shot this picture on a sofa that had once belonged to Marie Antoinette. She phoned me the next day and wanted to order lots of prints and asked me how much she owed me. I said, 'The pleasure that you have given me by liking my picture is payment enough.'

Well, after that she couldn't do enough for me. She'd take me through her attics and give me beautiful furniture. Those screens you used as a background to your portrait of me were a gift from Chanel. She bought them in East Africa.

She was the most amazing woman, with enormous talent. She invented everything that women wear today. I remember going round to dinner one night and finding her sewing the dress she was going to wear that evening. I asked her what she was doing. 'There's no one to sew my clothes,' she said, 'I have to do it myself.' She was quite wonderful. She would phone and say, 'Let's go to the movies and have a little dinner,' and I'd find myself at some film premiere with the President of France, followed by an enormous banquet.

After dinner, in her home in Paris, she would sit at a little card table by the fire with a group of friends like Cocteau and Dali. Some putty would be brought in, together with little bags of jewellery and precious stones – pearls, emeralds and diamenté – and she would sit there making models for her necklaces and brooches, sticking stones into the putty while the conversation went on around her. I remember once I was sitting playing with a piece of putty, kneading it in my hands. When I left I put it down on the card table. Two weeks later she had had it made into a silver lighter for me. That was the sort of person she was – so generous.

Chanel used to make the costumes for Cocteau's plays. At rehearsals she'd alter the clothes there and then, sitting on the stage, cutting and sewing. They were all innovators then – caring only about the end result, not about their egos.

Were you a little in love with her?

Yes. We had a very close relationship.

You often use famous people rather than professional models for your fashion pictures.

Yes. I think it adds another interesting dimension to the picture, but it took me a while to get over my shyness. One day I was photographing a princess. I had made the most beautiful flower arrangement – I knew it was superb because I'd copied it from a Cézanne painting. She stalked into the room and before she'd even said 'Hello', she told me to take the flowers away. 'I will have only white flowers,' she said.

Noël Coward taught me how to relax. He told me I shouldn't worry because the subjects themselves were so frightened by the camera that they hardly saw me. That really loosened me up. But you can hide behind the camera – Clare Luce showed me that. She had been drawing on a piece of paper during our session. Afterwards I asked her what she'd been doing – and she'd drawn a sketch of me. That made me feel very self-conscious.

One of the most beautiful models of her day was Lisa. Her looks were strikingly original. Later she was to marry Irving Penn. She loved modelling, but the girls in those days couldn't live off the income from it. I think they got 10 francs a day.

Courrèges Swimsuit, commission for French *Vogue*, Paris, c. 1979.

The lighting in your photographs is superb. What is your technique?

I like to use six small tungsten lights that I can carry around with me in a small aluminium suitcase. I can't stand using flash. Lighting is very important in the creation of mood because it adds drama and excitement to the photograph.

I took this photograph of a girl in a swimsuit quite recently, using lights from the old days. I was going to try shooting this picture with strobe, but I was unhappy about it because I can't see what I'm doing with strobe. In reality there's no such thing as the flat light it produces. I hate it – it's so unnatural. Anyway, I was rummaging through the equipment at French *Vogue* and I came across my old lights.

I put a strong spot about three feet away from the girl and a softer spot on the background, which I controlled with a barn door. I'm more concerned with shape than with anything else. You know, I don't think photography has anything remotely to do with the brain. It has to do with eye appeal.

That was my basic technique. The main tungsten light pointed at the subject a few feet away and I placed another tungsten spot theatre light of the same power a few feet further away, turning it slightly away from the subject. The first tungsten spot would give a glow to the picture and the second would provide the warmth and softness as a fill-in. Very simple. It's surprising what you can achieve with very little equipment. I'm all for using as little as I can.

You know it's funny – I've often tried to alter my technique, to experiment, but my pictures are always recognizable. I would build new sets and try different lighting, but the photographs always came out the same. You simply can't change the way you see things.

What made you leave Paris?

My lawyer told me I should go to America for political reasons, and he arranged for me to get an American passport instead of my German one. A lot of creative people had to leave Europe before the Second World War, although in the USA they'd hardly even heard of Van Gogh! I found myself staying in the same hotel as the novelist Vladimir Nabokov.

This photograph of the corset illustrates your fine lighting and your interest in shape. It also says something about your last hours in pre-war Europe.

This was a difficult picture to shoot. I'd never done a corset before. The lighting was quite complex. I can't remember how I did it and I certainly couldn't reproduce it now. It was the last picture I took in Paris before leaving on the *Normandie* for America. I remember I finished shooting the photograph at four in the morning and three hours later I was on the boat train. War broke out a few days later. There's a sort of moody sadness and eroticism apparent in this picture. A lot of feeling went into it. I was saying goodbye.

Did you print your own pictures?

No. French *Vogue* would do that, but I'd be there to control the image. When you look at an image you don't see every detail in sharp focus – you see some parts much more sharply than others. I like to emphasize that.

I used to re-touch my photographs a lot. This photograph of Paulette Goddard, for example, was re-touched to the waist. The hips were slimmed down and the laughter lines taken from the face. We had very few professional models in those days and their figures weren't as perfect as today's models.

Overleaf left: *The Corset,* Paris, c. 1936.

Overleaf right: *Paulette Goddard,* Rome, c. 1936.

116

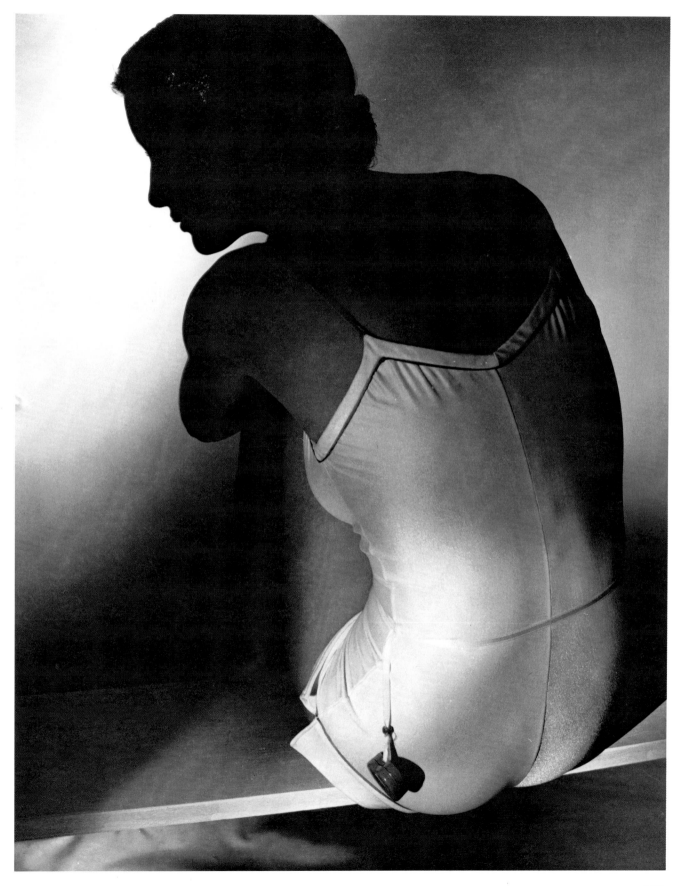

Goddard was a remarkably attractive woman. She was married to Erich Maria Remarque, the author of *All Quiet on the Western Front*. I'll never forget sitting between them in a sidewalk café on the Via Veneto in Rome – so many people, mainly American tourists, recognized her and came up to say 'Hello'.

Apart from lighting, how else did you achieve your effects?

I used to build a lot of sets. It would take me days to create them. Before the collections each year you never knew what was going to be produced, so you had to make several different types of set in case they didn't complement the creations. I'd make them out of boxes and bits of paper. This photograph is an example of what you can do with sets. I'd taken a picture of a 'society' woman wearing a hat but I found it an incredibly boring photograph. So I made an enlargement of the print and put the props in the picture after building a set.

What camera do you use?

In the old days we all followed Steichen, who was Condé Nast's favourite photographer, so I would use a 10 × 8 camera and artificial light. We weren't allowed to experiment and there were all sorts of rows about it. So we were limited to the big-format cameras, slow film and two- or three-second exposures. We also had to guess the light because there were no meters. Later I used a Rolleiflex with an ordinary lens. I still use that now, although recently I've been using a 35mm Nikon. It was such a revelation when Cartier-Bresson came along. The photographs he took were so revolutionary, so marvellously liberated.

How do you get on with art directors and fashion editors? I know you had a stormy relationship with Condé Nast.

Yes, we had a terrible row. One day he was sitting down with an art director and he had all my photographs on his desk. They were both criticizing them and I was defending them. Eventually he said with great sarcasm, 'I suppose you think you're as good as Steichen,' who was his god. I replied, 'If I didn't think I could be as good as Steichen one day, I wouldn't bother to take photographs.' I suppose, looking back, I said it with rather an arrogant, youthful air. Well, Mr Nast blew his top and said, 'When your contract is up, leave us.' I said, 'I won't be told when to leave. I'll leave tomorrow.' And I did.

But that was nothing compared to the behaviour of George Hoyningen-Huene, my great friend and, incidentally, the man who taught me everything I know about photography. While he was working in New York for *Harper's Bazaar* he was taken out to lunch by the same art director who had been with Condé Nast at the time of our argument. The art director was buttering him up, saying things like, 'Oh, George, you're the most marvellous photographer, the only one. We love your work more than that of any other photographer. But really, George, you know you must behave – no more tantrums.'

George picked up the plate of food in front of him and said, 'Yes, you are quite right. I must behave. No more bad behaviour, I promise.' Then he dumped his plate of food in the art director's lap. He really was an *enfant terrible*.

I still hate working with an art director. So often they see the picture in a totally different way. It may be one hundred per cent right for them, but it's not for me. Sometimes they'll walk into my picture to pull at a frill or straighten a belt. That drives me mad. Pulling something straight can lose the whole picture.

Still-Life with Hat and Quill, New York, *c.* 1936.

121

For a time you gave up fashion photography and started to photograph interiors.

Yes, that was when Diana Vreeland came along, and we didn't get on very well. I was getting a bit tired of fashion photography, so I thought I'd try taking interiors. Actually it was a great success. The interiors were taking up so much of my time that, stupidly, I gave up my studio. The moment I did, they fired Diana Vreeland. Still, I did a lot of good work for *House and Garden*. I liked the editor there very much. The most important point about photographing interiors is not to try to show the whole thing all at once. You must pick out some particular aspect of the room and emphasize it, to give the viewer the sensation of what it might be like to live there. That's the secret, and it's the same with fashion.

Tell me about the Marlene Dietrich picture.

This photograph of her was taken for *Vogue*. It was part of the 'Bundles for Britain' campaign. Different manufacturers would set aside and advertise some of their garments, and the proceeds from the sales would go to help the British war effort. That was in the days before America had entered the war and Britain stood alone against Germany.

What do you feel about your pictures selling for high prices?

I love it. When the galleries first started to sell the prints we had no idea how valuable they would be. I always used to throw the prints away. Now I get my assistant and a girl from Sotheby's to file the negatives so they can be found easily. French *Vogue* threw out most of the negatives of my 1930s' fashion photographs. Only a few remain.

In the old days photography wasn't considered one of the arts. I knew so many of the great artists of those days – Picasso, Matisse, Miró – and none of them thought photography was particularly important. They certainly admired the work of Atget and Cartier-Bresson, but I don't think anybody collected it. Gertrude Stein certainly didn't.

But it was so exciting living in Paris then. It was a real community of artists – Cocteau, Bérard, Dali and many others – and we were all so interested in each other's work. It was a great source of inspiration to me. Of course it's very different now with artists scattered all over the place in Paris, New York and London. Even in New York some artists live on Seventh Avenue and others in the Hamptons.

Wasn't Man Ray a great friend of yours in those days?

Yes. I used to call him the 'dark-room photographer'. He was much more interested in manipulating the film than in taking photographs. I was quite the opposite, a traditionalist.

How would you sum up your attitude to your work?

I find it difficult to analyze my pictures, either when I'm creating the image or in retrospect. They certainly have that strong personal stamp – I don't know why and I don't really care. That's for others to say. I'm not interested in analysis. I regard myself as a craftsman rather than an artist, though people can call me an artist if they wish.

The most important thing is to keep changing, to develop and do different things. The problem is that people begin to think about you in a particular way and you become categorized as a certain type of photographer. I'd like to experiment and explore new themes in the same way that in the past I started, almost by chance, to take interiors. Unfortunately nobody asks me.

Marlene Dietrich,
commission for English
Vogue, New York, *c.* 1935.

Yousuf Karsh

Yousuf Karsh was born in Armenia in 1908. Now a Canadian citizen living in Ottawa, he is the world's most famous portrait photographer. He escaped the horrors of the Turkish massacres of the Armenian minority when his family fled to Syria. Three years later, in 1924, he went to Canada, and shortly afterwards began his career in photography. He first studied in Massachussetts with the photographer John Garo, and opened his own studio in Ottawa in 1932.

As he began to establish himself he would photograph the famous who visited Ottawa. In 1941 his friend and patron, Prime Minister Mackenzie King, arranged for him to photograph Winston Churchill at the time when England stood alone against Nazi Germany. The portrait catapulted Karsh to international fame. It was published on the cover of *Life* magazine, and the same photograph was to be used on stamps for seven different countries.

Since that time Karsh's international reputation has grown rapidly and famous men and women from all walks of life consider a sitting with him the ultimate accolade. His portrait of President Kennedy was on the cover of *Life*'s memorial issue and he was the first to take official portraits of Nikita Kruschev and members of the Soviet Praesidium. He has photographed the British Royal Family, Pope John Paul II and people as diverse as Albert Einstein, Ernest Hemingway, George Bernard Shaw, Pablo Picasso, Pablo Casals, Carl Jung, Rogers and Hammerstein, Jawaharlal Nehru, Albert Schweitzer, John Steinbeck, Sibelius, Stravinsky, Thomas Mann, President Eisenhower, Bertrand Russell, Eleanor Roosevelt and Martin Luther King.

Karsh himself describes his mission as 'to photograph the great in heart, in mind and in spirit, whether they be famous or humble', and his photographic contributions to the cause of handicapped children earned him, in 1971, a Presidential Citation in the USA. In 1975 he presented his collection of medical and scientific personalities, *Healers of Our Age*, to the Harvard and Boston Medical Libraries.

Karsh's photographs feature in the permanent collections at the Metropolitan Museum and the Museum of Modern Art in New York, the Art Institute of Chicago, and the National Portrait Gallery in London. He has exhibited widely throughout the world, notably in his one-man exhibition at the National Gallery of Canada in 1959, and the

'Look and think before opening the shutter. The heart and mind are the true lens of the camera.'

Men Who Make Our World show at *Expo 67*, which travelled all over the USA and Europe.

Karsh is generous in his help to aspiring photographers, and a frequent teacher at photographic workshops in America. He was Visiting Professor of Photography at Ohio University and in 1972 was appointed Visiting Professor of Fine Arts at Emerson College, Boston, Massachusetts.

Karsh works on the sixth floor of the Château Laurier Hotel in Ottawa. There is a reception area and an ante-room, on the walls of which hang huge prints of some of his most famous portraits, including those of Churchill, Georgia O'Keefe and Queen Elizabeth II. The working studio area is a long, thin alcove, two walls of which are painted cream and the third black.

Today Karsh travels the world with his wife, taking his unique photographs of famous and interesting people. His photographs make use of the subject's own natural environment and concentrate on the eyes and hands to capture the essence of the sitter's personality. His tried and trusted technique ensure portraits that are honest and straightforward, often of a sombre simplicity that cuts through all superficiality to reveal the subject's mind.

'Look and think before opening the shutter. The heart and mind are the true lens of the camera.' His own dictum is the best summary of his art.

———•———

What made you take up photography?

Actually, I always wanted to be a doctor. I was born in Armenia and came to Canada in 1924 to go to medical school. My Uncle Nakash arranged for me to come here and I'd hoped he'd put me through college. But he was not as wealthy as I thought, so financially I was on my own. However he did a great deal for me. He gave me my first camera, a Box Brownie, and encouraged me to take photographs. When I was seventeen he sent a picture of mine to a photographic competition and I won first prize of $50. I remember I sent $40 to my family in Armenia and kept the rest for myself. That was really the beginning of my photographic career, because it encouraged me to think that I'd be able to support myself at it. I abandoned all ideas of medicine.

That wasn't the end of my uncle's influence. He was very supportive of my photographic ambitions and he arranged for me to go to Boston to work with a photographer friend of his, John Garo. I studied with him for three wonderful years. I learned a lot about photography and a lot about life.

What did you learn from Garo about portraiture?

He was extraordinarily talented. He used only natural daylight in his studio and in my early years I did the same. Later I discovered the possibilities of tungsten. I was about twenty-four at the time and I'd go to the theatre workshop where my first wife worked as an actress. I'd go to see her perform and was profoundly impressed by the lighting techniques they used. The artistic quality was extremely high. They could produce different moods at will merely by changing the lighting. Nothing seemed to be impossible.

I started to work on my own technique from that time, using tungsten lights I made at home. It's tremendously important to find your own style by endless experimentation, which is why I never lecture students on lighting. You have to discover it for yourself. Once you have, you carry on with it, developing it, until it satisfies you. There are no short cuts. My own lighting is very basic, very simple, but of course I modify it slightly to suit the different needs of the individual subjects. You never truly master the technique of lighting. That's its fascination. There's always something new to learn.

In my studio I use tungsten floods or spots, although I always use electronic lighting when I'm away from the studio – which is most of the time. Sometimes I combine flash with daylight.

Can we talk about some of these portraits that hang on the walls of your studio? Perhaps we could start with Churchill.

This photograph signalled the beginning of my international career and it was a frightening experience. I had exactly four minutes to take the picture. I like to meet or at least to see the subject of a portrait before the session, so I'd made a point of listening to the address that Churchill was giving to the Canadian Parliament before hurrying back to the Speaker's chamber where I'd set up my lighting. The speech was an important one – the 'some chicken, some neck' speech – and it gave me a pretty clear idea of Churchill's personality. It was certainly not an ideal situation: when he came out it appeared that nobody had warned him there would be a photo session and he only allowed me to take a single photograph. After I'd removed the cigar from his mouth he positively exuded belligerence. That's what I think the photograph captures – the essence of England in those days, unbeaten and unbowed. Later he paid me a great compliment: he said I had the power to still the roaring lion!

Do you always manage to take your subjects in four minutes?

No. But sometimes the longer you have with a subject the less able you are to get a powerful shot. I was in the Oval Office with President Carter for three hours, for example, and I've never been satisfied with the results. I've never published those photographs in any of my books, either.

How important is getting to know your subject before the sitting?

Very. I like to prepare myself and to research the subject for several reasons. If I've made the effort to find out all about the sitter beforehand, it enables me to build rapport, which helps to reveal the personality. Also I'm extremely privileged to meet the most fascinating people through my work and I'm naturally interested to find out about them, their motivation and their feelings. Research is essential if you're to establish a good relationship.

Tell me about the portrait of Georgia O'Keefe.

I photographed her in Abiquiu, New Mexico, in 1956. The most interesting facet of her personality was her incredible dedication to her work and the stark austerity of her approach to it. She has no time to spare for people, not because she doesn't like them, but because she loves her painting more, and every moment spent with people means less time for her art. My portrait had to reflect those qualities – simplicity, austerity, dedication – so I caught her in profile, making a point of her strong hands. White hands against the black dress give the impression of calm serenity, and yet her determination comes across as well.

You obviously admired her very much.

Yes. I was tremendously impressed by her single-mindedness and her powers of concentration. With her, too, there was that meeting of minds without which it's very difficult to take a really great portrait.

Overleaf left: *Winston Churchill*, Canadian Parliament, *c.* 1941.

Overleaf right: *Georgia O'Keefe*, Abiquiu, New Mexico, 1956.

You must have achieved that rapport with Helen Keller, despite her disabilities.

She was the most spiritually uplifting woman I've ever met. An inner light seemed to shine from her. She'd been totally blind and deaf from earliest childhood, but her outstanding quality, even more than her kindness and understanding, was her gaiety. When I first met her she ran her hands over my face so she could see me in her mind. Later I was able to communicate with her and direct the sitting by the very slightest pressure of my finger tips on her palms. All the lost powers of sight and hearing had passed into her hands, so it was just as important to capture them in the portrait as it was to record the image of her face.

Tell me about your famous portrait of Pablo Casals.

This photograph was shot in the Abbey of St Miguel de Cuxa. The only light source in the dark, dingy room was a single electric bulb, though luckily I was able to find a power source for my strobe unit. All through the session Casals played the most sublime music on his cello while I worked around him. It was a magical experience. Suddenly

Helen Keller, New York, 1948.

Opposite: *Pablo Casals*, Prades, 1954.

131

I decided to experiment and take a photograph from behind him. I think this portrait captures the immense physical and spiritual power that flowed from this genius of a musician.

Do you ever work in colour?

I prefer not to, although I often repeat a black-and-white portrait in colour if there's time. I find colour more difficult to control. It's not so easy to imprint your own artistic style on the picture. You can't change your mind, as it were. You're at the mercy of Kodak's laboratory. I think these pictures should be called Kodak reproductions, not the photographer's. If I do use colour it's usually Kodachrome or Ektachrome, most often 64 ASA.

What equipment do you use?

Usually a 10×8 – often a 5×4 view camera. For 35mm work I use a Leica. In the past I've often used a Rolleiflex. I use Tri-X 400 film for the black-and-white portraits, although I'm very dissatisfied with the printing paper that's available nowadays. It has many limitations. I always develop my own film. In my small dark-room I have a device that allows me to gauge from the negative the degree of exposure, from which I can deduce the optimum degree of development. It looks like a long shoe box with the top removed and replaced with two pieces of glass, one for $2\frac{1}{4}$ square film and the other for 5×4 or 10×8. There's a green filter across the front of the box. After exposure I soften up the film in a water bath. Then it gets two minutes in a Kodak desensitizer, which is kept at an average temperature of 68 degrees. After removing the negative from the desensitizer I hold it up to the light box to assess the development it needs. This is the vital stage, and because it's so important I never delegate the responsibility.

Do you use exposure meters?

I read them from time to time, but I only *use* them if they agree with what I judge to be the right exposure.

So you favour simplicity and straightforwardness in technique?

Yes. Very great photographs can be taken using simple cameras and daylight. There's much more to taking a good portrait than mere technique. You must have an understanding of people, of why they do things. You must learn to recognize their essential qualities and know how to capture them. You must be able to get on with your subject. When you are in possession of all these qualities, then and only then you can take a photograph.

You should also be totally at home with your equipment through constant practice. Your methods must be right for others. That's why I'm never very keen to dwell on my methods and techniques. It's not that I'm secretive about them, merely that they're vitally important to me. There's no substitute for practice. You only find out about people and how to use cameras through trial and error. That's the only way to discover your own individuality. It's more important to know about life than about photographic technique in portraiture. And using the camera must become second nature. You shouldn't have to think too much about it.

Which photographers do you most admire?

Garo, of course. But Steichen was the greatest force, without a doubt. He was a close friend. However I think that Stieglitz was the greater artist.

Your prints are now very valuable. How do you deal with that?

I keep all my negatives in a fireproof bank vault. Arson is very popular in Ottawa! I keep some prints in my archives here, but they haven't been properly fixed, so they have to be kept in the dark most of the time or they'll be lost. Like this one of Jean Cocteau, for example – it even has his spidery signature on the back.

You've taken many pictures of the British Royal Family and they're great admirers of your work. What do you think of the work of a 'royal' photographer like Patrick Lichfield?

I had dinner with him on my last visit to London. I have great respect for him both as a photographer and as a man. I find it amazing that he's been able to overcome the obstacle to his professional career of being a cousin of the Queen.

As we walked around Ottawa this afternoon many people came up to speak to you. What do you feel about fame – your own and other people's?

I am known here because Ottawa is very small, like a village – a wonderful place. I *am* fascinated by what makes people great. It seems that great talent isn't enough. There must be something else – inspiration, dedication. You get a sense of it from people, but it's very intangible. I suppose it's a sort of inner strength that communicates itself and leaves its mark. Those who possess it may be a little arrogant and usually competitive but they share a curiosity, the search for truth. I'm tremendously pleased to have had the chance to meet so many of the most interesting and forceful people of our age. Not many others have had that opportunity.

André Kertész

André Kertész was born a Hungarian citizen in Budapest in 1894, and educated at the Chamber of Commerce there. From 1912 to 1914 and again from 1918 to 1925 he worked as a clerk in the Budapest Stock Exchange. In 1914 he joined the Austro-Hungarian Army in Poland and in the following year he was wounded in the First World War. From about the age of fourteen Kertész had been interested in photography and during the war he took a camera, a Goetz Tenax, into the front line.

Kertész sought to record the commonplace events, the 'little happenings', and, in using his camera like a pen, to keep a diary of life as he saw it. He showed no interest in the frenetic social life of the Hungarian capital. He preferred to photograph less obvious occurrences, whose significance was no less profound and no less characteristic of the times.

In 1925 he went to Paris to work as a freelance photographer for such magazines as *Frankfurter Illustrierte, Uhu, Vu, Le Sourire, La Nazionale di Fiorenza,* and for the London *Times*. Kertész, captivated by the atmosphere of Paris and stimulated by its exciting artistic environment, befriended painters like Chagall, Mondrian and Vlaminck. His work found ready acceptance among sophisticated Parisians, who appreciated his ability to 'see' images often invisible to less artistically creative eyes. He had his first exhibition in 1927 at the Galerie Le Sacré du Printemps and was invited to show his work in the First Independent Salon of Photography.

His great contribution to photography was his invention of the photo-reportage style, a contribution acknowledged by his friend Cartier-Bresson when he said, 'We all owe something to Kertész.' By his intuitive use of the small-format camera to draw attention to little regarded or unrecognized aspects of everyday life, Kertész paved the way for a whole new movement in photography. In particular Brassaï, acute observer of Parisian street life, learned his art from his friend and mentor Kertész.

Stimulated by Surrealist influences in the Paris of the late 1920s and early 1930s, Kertész experimented, and in his 'nude distortion' series refined and developed a process begun in Hungary many years before – and to which he has returned more recently in New York. These pictures show an abstract quality transcending his intuitively observed reality.

'My talent lies in the fact that I cannot touch a camera without expressing myself.'

In 1936, against the advice of his wife, Elizabeth, whom he had married in 1933, he left Paris for New York to work for a year as a contract photographer for Keystone Studios, a major picture agency. It was a move he has always bitterly regretted. Financial difficulties and the impending outbreak of war combined to prevent Kertész's return to the Paris he had come to love. The Americans failed to understand the true extent of his genius. It was 1937 and Edward Weston was the man of the moment in American photography; the large-format camera, rather than the 35mm, was their favoured instrument. *Life* magazine, the show-place of American photography, failed to publish his work. So Kertész worked freelance, primarily for Condé Nast, from 1937 to 1949, and subsequently on contract to Condé Nast from 1949 to 1962.

Although five of his photographs were exhibited in the *Photographers, 1848–1937* exhibition at the Museum of Modern Art, it was not until 1946 that he had a one-man show at the Art Institute of Chicago. When the far-seeing and enlightened John Szarkowski mounted the major one-man retrospective at MOMA in 1964, Kertész's monumental contribution to modern photography was finally recognized.

His one-man exhibitions include shows at the Galerie Le Sacré du Printemps, Paris, in 1927; the Art Institute of Chicago, in 1946; Long Island University, New York, in 1962; the Bibliothèque Nationale, Paris, and the Modern Age Studio, New York, both in 1963; the Museum of Modern Art, New York, in 1964; the Moderna Museet, Stockholm, and the Magyar Neuzeta Galeria, Budapest, both in 1971; the Valokuvamuseum, Helsinki, in 1972; the Hallmark Gallery, New York, and the Light Gallery, New York, both in 1973; Wesleyan University, Middletown, Connecticut, and the French Cultural Institute, New York, both in 1976; the Musée d'Art Moderne, Centre Beaubourg, Paris, in 1977; *Sympathetic Explorations*, at the Plains Art Museum, Morehead, Minnesota, also in 1977; the Serpentine Gallery, London, in 1979; Salford University, England, and the Israel Museum, Jerusalem, both in 1980.

Kertész lives today in New York City, where he works as a freelance. He has been his own master since 1962, free at last, as in Parisian days, to unleash the full force of his genius. Recently poor health has confined him to his apartment overlooking Washington Square, but it has not lessened the power of his vision. He has suffered for his art, but, uncompromising, unyielding in his pursuit of his artistic ideals, he has never lost his way. His reputation as the father of modern photography is now secure.

When and how did you start taking photographs?

It was a very long time ago – I know I bought my first proper camera, an ICA 'Baby', in 1912. Before that I had a cheap box camera, but I forget the make. Then I had an Ernemann pocket camera. I took my first photograph as early as 1900 when I was six years old. All my family had cameras and my first photograph was taken at a gathering of relatives. I found some old calendars and some of the images were of beautiful old family scenes. They were so sentimental and their simplicity influenced me. I'm a great sentimentalist – I always have been.

I started to think of photography about three or four years before I bought the ICA, visualizing the pictures in my mind. When I was composing the pictures mentally, I knew for certain that I could achieve what I wanted in photography. That feeling has never left me. It's a gift that I have – totally instinctive. I always know, creatively, that I'm doing the right thing.

The ICA had twelve negatives, 6×4.5cm glass plates, and only one shutter speed so you could never guarantee the image. Most professional photographers used only large-format cameras with a tripod, but I wanted to move around as much as possible and so I bought the small camera.

The technical side of photography was a complete mystery to me, a real puzzle. I just had to work it out for myself by experimenting. My dark-room was never dark enough, for instance, but it never worried me. I persevered. The technical side of photography is only meaningful if it enhances your art. Good technique on its own is meaningless. A child may have beautiful writing but it's *what* he writes that's important. In my interpretation the Group f/64 were people who had learned to perfect the calligraphy of the medium. They could produce the alphabet of photography beautifully. They were calligraphic photographers. I, on the other hand, have never been obsessed with sharpness or with depth of field. My pictures are constantly on the move, in the same way as life itself.

I admire your early pictures – the ones taken around Budapest. I particularly like this one of the naked man by the riverside.

It's a photograph of my brother. A few years ago the Hungarian Government put on an exhibition for me and I was able to go back and visit all the old places. But they'd changed so much I hardly recognized them.

André Kertész

Lagymanyos, October 7th 1919, Budapest, 1919.

137

Distortion, Number 91 and Self-Portrait, Paris, 1933.

What did you think of Paris when you first went there?

That was in 1925, and I loved it. There were never any restrictions placed on me there – not at all like New York. I became great friends with many of the painters, such as Chagall and Mondrian. I shot this picture in Mondrian's studio. I'm very proud of it. I positioned myself behind the sofa, which was an unusual vantage point, and I got the exact photograph that I'd composed in my mind. Mondrian was a great friend – he liked my pictures very much.

What sort of work did you do in Paris?

I worked freelance for Condé Nast for a bit. In 1928 I bought my first Leica. That made a big difference. I'd take it with me wherever I went, taking shots of people when they weren't looking. This new style of photography was very much the thing for the illustrated news magazines which were just beginning. They'd commission me and let me do what I wanted. Take the nudes, for example. In 1933 I was asked by Monsieur Querelle, the proprietor of a 'girlie' magazine, *Le Sourire*, to take some photographs of nudes. He was rather embarrassed to ask me – I think he thought I might consider it beneath my dignity. Actually I didn't mind at all. The great thing was he gave me absolute freedom to do what I liked. I'd used the distorting power of water in some photographs of a swimmer, so I got hold of a fairground distorting mirror and these nudes are the result. I think they're very original. I shot them all in the course of a single month.

One of them has me in the photograph and I meant it to double as a self-portrait. I don't think anybody has reproduced this photograph with me in the picture before. They usually crop me out!

Opposite: *Chez Mondrian*, Paris, 1926.

Opposite: *Distortion, Number 70*, Paris, 1933.

In 1937 you went to New York but it wasn't a success. What went wrong?

I was treated miserably – cheated. I had met a man called Ernie Prince who suggested I take a sabbatical and go to New York for a year. When I told my wife what I was intending to do she said, 'André, if you do I'll divorce you.' I am glad to say she didn't. I loved her very much. But I wished I'd listened to her.

I was working as a reporter in Paris at the time and thought that I'd do reportage when I got to New York. But instead Prince asked me to do the most ordinary commercial work that I've ever seen. I said, 'I'm a reporter, not a commercial artist.' But what could I do? I had no money to return to Paris, otherwise I would have done so like a shot. Just before I left they'd paid me the great compliment of offering me French citizenship on the basis of artistic merit.

Distortion, Number 120, Paris, 1933.

Anyway, I couldn't go back, so I did these commercial assignments and – can you believe it? – Prince ran off with my money. Finally, Dr Agha of Condé Nast telephoned

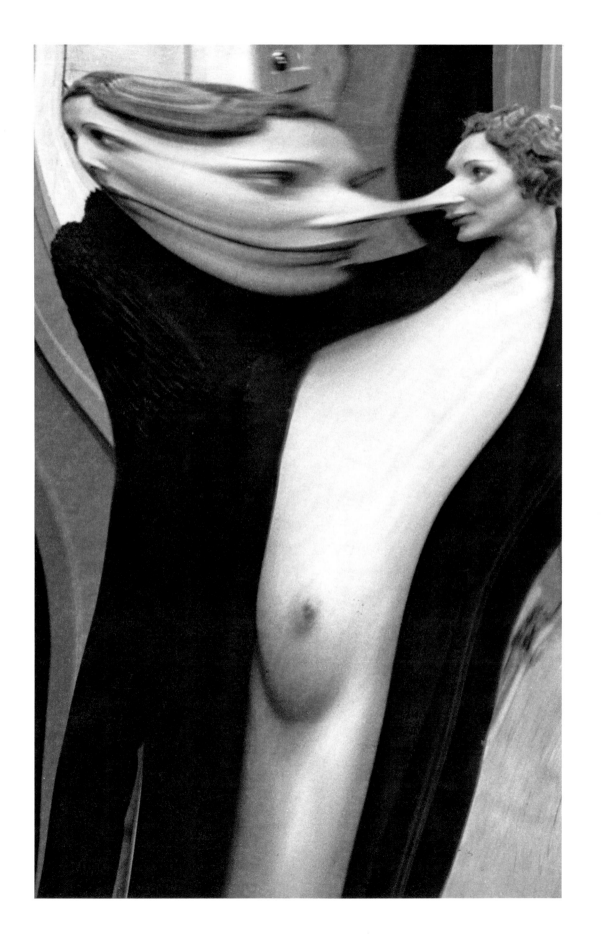

me when he heard I was working with this man and warned me that he was a charlatan. But by then it was too late. I had nothing to live on, so I had to do commercial work for another eight months just to survive. Some of my pictures actually came out in *Life* magazine in 1933 with Prince's name underneath! Amazing!

Before that, in Paris, I'd only done what I call spiritual fashion, never direct fashion. What hurts so much is that before the war I was so well respected in Paris. I was considered a great artist. The moment I arrived in America I was treated like a cheap commercial photographer. I'll never forgive them for that.

The Americans took a long time to respect photographers who worked with small-format cameras, and although in the late 1930s the galleries were starting to collect photographs they were wary of anything that wasn't taken on a 10×8. They wanted all photographs to look like Edward Weston's. He used large-format cameras and small apertures, and gave long exposures – so the pictures were very sharp and had great depth of field. I wasn't impressed by those qualities. I was more interested in capturing and expressing the feel of the moment. In life things are often not very sharp, not very clear. I'm a complete realist. I like to record things as they are, and that may be a little soft and blurred. Take my nudes, for example. They're certainly distorted, but they are true reflections of reality. People have talked as if I was a Surrealist, but I'm not that at all.

Anyway it took the Americans a long time to understand the value of my photographs. At *Life* magazine they said, 'Yes, André, we like your photographs, but you're inclined to talk too much in them.' They wanted technique, not creative photography. To my mind the only reportage photographer that America has ever produced is Eugene Smith. He was the only intelligent reporter.

You must learn all you can about technique and then forget it. You should use the minimum amount that enables you to express yourself.

Clearly you dislike technique for technique's sake. How would you characterize your own qualities as a photographer?

My talent lies in the fact that I cannot touch a camera without expressing myself. An art critic once wrote of my book *Washington Square*, 'Washington Square only looks nice if you happen to be André Kertész looking down on it.' I like looking down on a subject because then you see everything, but you must not be too high. The idea for the *Washington Square* series came from a French publication called *Du*. They published an issue which was called *From my Window in Washington Square* – or something like that.

Do you shoot a lot of film?

No. That would be using the camera in a chance way. The moment dictates when I should take a photograph. If it's not right then I don't take the picture. When I see a good situation I know it at once. Sometimes I wait for a few days to capture an image because the first time I see it the light may not be exactly right. I think it's a problem for many young American photographers that they take three hundred shots to get two. The only way I can express it is to use an old Hungarian proverb. The blind chicken goes around his pen picking and feeling for corn and maybe eventually he'll pick up a grain. Most of the time, however, he'll get only small pebbles in his beak. The chicken who can see will only pick up grain. It's a case of whether or not you can see. Many people look but few see. I always think of the time I was having my 1927 Paris exhibition – the Dadaists were handing out stickers which said, 'You who do not see please spare a thought for those who can.'

Washington Square, January 9th 1954, New York, 1954.

143

Why didn't you return to Paris when you could?

When I'd scraped together enough money it was just before the Second World War, and it was too late to return to Europe. They made me an enemy alien, you know. They actually finger-printed me and I was only allowed to photograph inside America. Outside America I was considered a spy!

After the war a friend of mine called Alex Lieberman became art adviser to Condé Nast and he asked me to help him change the look of *House and Garden*. At first I said 'No', but then I relented because they promised to publish my own personal pictures later on. It was terrible for me to take pictures that I didn't want to take. It was so bad that I cancelled my contract with Condé Nast, but circumstances dictated that I had to work for others. I nearly killed myself. I certainly thought of suicide. That was how bad it was for me to have to compromise my artistic beliefs.

I remember one particular occasion when Alex sent me with a designer to shoot some interiors for *House and Garden*. It took me three days to take those pictures. When I showed them to Alex he said, 'Wonderful, André. Now go back and take them again, but this time shoot ordinary, commercial pictures.' I said, 'Why don't you find some-body in the street to shoot these pictures? Anybody could do them.' I did the re-shoot. Then I told him I never wanted to see him again.

But after all those years they haven't forgotten you in Paris, have they?

Even today I'm constantly invited back by the Creative Arts Council. I was there recently and the Mayor of Paris gave me a medal. He made a beautiful speech and called me '*le plus Parisien*' photographer. 'You were born Hungarian,' he said, 'and now you're an American citizen, but your blood and your heart are French.' It touched me greatly.

Do you work through a gallery now?

No. I worked with the Light Gallery for a while, because after 1962 I decided not to do any more commercial work. Now I live mostly off the sale of my pictures, but I don't get on with dealers. I'm not a commercial man. I've made considerable financial sacrifices for my work.

I notice you collect glass objects.

Yes. I've used them to work with in a new book of Polaroid pictures that I'm doing. I don't collect rare glass, only ordinary popular glass. Since ill health has confined me to the house I've found I've been able to make some remarkably good distorted photographs by shooting through the glass objects. They'll appear in a book that Polaroid are going to publish in 1983. I like these images very much. I shoot through glass frogs and fishes. In Budapest I did similar pictures using household glass, but all those negatives were lost or destroyed in the occupation.

You must admit that today you've gained the recognition denied you for so many years.

Yes. John Szarkowski is really responsible. He put on my 1964 one-man show at the Museum of Modern Art. And do you know, people asked me where I'd been all these years!

J. H. Lartigue

Jacques-Henri Lartigue, the son of wealthy parents, was born at Courbevoie near Paris in 1894. His father, a keen amateur photographer, encouraged his son's interest in photography, giving him his first camera in 1901, when the young Lartigue was only seven years old. His was a sheltered, privileged childhood, with a private tutor. A large, boisterous family of cousins gave him the opportunity to capture for posterity the atmosphere of carefree, fun-loving excitement that characterized a *fin de siècle* childhood.

'I have never taken a picture for any other reason than that at that moment it made me happy to do so.'

Lartigue's photographs, however, are far more than a fascinating social documentation of those distant times. From his earliest days he was intrigued by the new inventions that were irretrievably changing the face of society. The motor car, the aeroplane, the motorized bicycle filled him with excitement. He had only a still camera, but it was his remarkable achievement to capture movement on film. A dare-devil cousin careers down a steep incline on a machine that Lartigue himself helped to design, an ungainly kite takes uncertainly to the air, an umbrella is plucked by the wind from the hand of a pretty girl — and Lartigue is there to record it.

In the early photographs, too, another life-long interest of Lartigue's is apparent. It is obvious from the delicate way that he handles his subject matter that Lartigue is a lover of women — the pretty cousin, Simone, and the tender photograph of his mother, merge into the closely observed fine ladies at the races or in the Bois de Boulogne. His women are often distant, imposing, secure behind the barricades of 'fancy' clothes and exotic hats. At other times they are charmingly natural, running, jumping, playing and always laughing, active and happy. Lartigue greatly admired his cousin Simone because she knew how to play and she played hard — qualities that he greatly respects. In his later photographs his interest in women is no less keen, but the focus changes in the almost reverent studies of the beautiful Renée and the ethereal Solange, and then alters again in the self-conscious glamour of the young Senator Kennedy's poolside companion. 'I only photograph images that make me happy,' says Lartigue. Obviously women have the power to do just that.

Few photographers' work has retained such consistent brilliance over so long a period but, remarkably, it is only relatively recently that Lartigue has received international recognition. For most of his life it was as a painter that he was acclaimed: he had a considerable reputation and was a friend of Van Dongen, Cocteau, Picasso and Colette.

When he was fifty, his photographs were seen by chance in New York and his phenomenal talent was immediately recognized. In 1963 he was given a major one-man show at the Museum of Modern Art in New York. Richard Avedon saw the exhibition, bought some of the prints, and, in 1970, edited the famous book of Lartigue's photographs, *Diary of a Century*.

Today few would dispute that Lartigue is a seminal figure in the history of photography who ranks with the very greatest practitioners of the medium. His zest and enthusiasm for life remain, his optimism undimmed by advancing years. When he was a child he saw with the eyes of the most perceptive of men. Now he brings to his old age the fresh and innocent vision of the child. In June 1979 he donated his entire

collection to the French state. The non-profit-making organization Friends of Jacques-Henri Lartigue exists to protect and preserve his photographic work, which is on permanent exhibition at the Grand Palais des Champs-Elysées. Lartigue's one-man exhibitions have included shows at the Museum of Modern Art, New York, in 1963, and the Photographers' Gallery, London, in 1971.

J.-H. Lartigue

———•———

You were once known mainly as a painter. Which medium do you prefer?

Both painting and photography are important to me. I started both at the same time. One could not see the results of a photograph immediately and so I would sketch the images that I had shot to remind myself of them. In this photograph, which is a self-portrait, you see me in my garden doing both. I had my first exhibition of paintings when I was eighteen. Of course I wasn't 'discovered' as a photographer until I was fifty.

Autoportrait, Rouzat, 1923.

J.-H. Lartigue

Simone Roussel.

How did your work get 'discovered'?

It was quite by chance. I had decided to take a trip around the world with my wife, Florette. We were in New York where we didn't know a soul and Florette wanted to get some pictures retouched, so a friend gave us the name of a man who owned a photographic agency. When he saw these photographs of mine he became very excited and asked if anybody had seen the pictures before. We said, 'Yes, of course – family, friends. Sometimes we show them after dinner.' After that, all is history. The Museum of Modern Art gave me an exhibition, and a young man called Richard Avedon came to see it and bought some of the prints. That was in 1963. In 1967 he came to visit us in Paris and I showed him my albums. They were not really albums, but pages three feet long on which I had laid out my photographs and sketches. Richard took them back to New York with him and produced *Diary of a Century*. You know it's funny – for twenty years I had been showing my pictures to people, but until that book and the New York exhibition in a way nobody had seen them before.

When, in fact, did you take your first photographs?

It was in 1901 and I used my father's camera. My own first camera was a large wooden box, highly polished. I would have to make the exposures standing on a chair. I would time the exposure by counting up to three.

It appears that you had a very happy childhood. How did you get on at school?

I never went to school. In those days it was not obligatory and I had a tutor who would come to the house. I suppose you might say that I had a very privileged upbringing. I never felt lonely as a child, because there was always a lot going on and there were always masses of people around. Funnily enough, though, I was never particularly fond of people of my own age. I always liked either babies or very old people. I'm still like that today, only it is not easy to find anyone older than me!

My special friend was my dare-devil cousin, Simone, who would come to visit us on Sundays. She was lovely, and such fun. She was the only friend I had who was prepared to play without talking! I made this two-wheeler machine by cutting one of our bob-sleds in half.

My brother Maurice was a great inventor. He even tried to build his own flying machine. He also invented a kind of boat. You would slip your legs into waders sealed to the bottom of this rubber ring and literally walk through water.

Zissou à Rouzat, Rouzat, 1911.

Papa et Maman, Pont de
l'Arche, 1902.

You were the very first person to capture movement in photography.

Yes. I was especially fascinated by flight, but any movement was fun.

Your pictures exude great optimism and happiness. How have you managed this?

I think I have retained the thoughts of a child, but that is God-given. I am a very happy
man, and a light-hearted one, so I guess my pictures reflect the kind of man I am. I have
only ever painted or taken photographs for my own pleasure, never anybody else's, and
I don't care how the world sees me.

Your signature with the big sun after your name is intriguing. How did it evolve?

When I was a child it seemed to me that the sun always shone, and when I wrote notes
to my elder brother I would always draw a sun after my name.

Do you have a favourite photograph?

No. I like many of them. This is the first photograph I ever took of my parents. They
posed for me in the garden of our house. They decided on their position, but I told them
not to move. I directed them.

Opposite: *Cerf Volant*,
Biarritz, 1905.

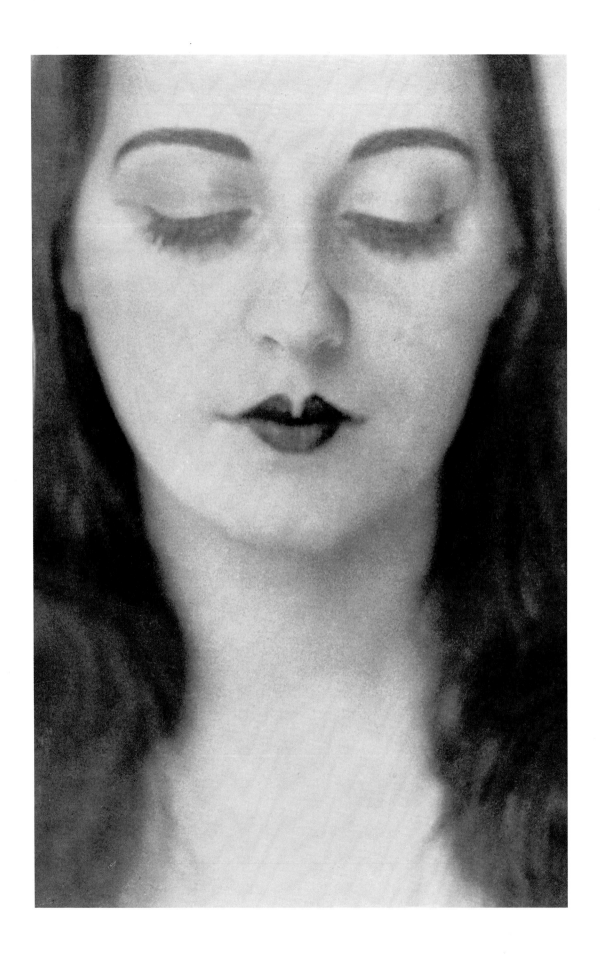

It seems that women have been a major force in your life.

Renée, Paris, 1931.

I like more than anything in the world to be happy, and women help me to be happy. I am fond of them as friends and lovers. You know, I only take photographs of what I like, and the thing that pleases me most to look at is a woman. I have never taken a picture for any other reason than that at that moment it made me happy to do so. You see, I have never been one to analyze too deeply either my motives or those of others.

What about your technique and working methods – do you use a lot of film to get one shot?

No. That is a matter of discipline. You see, when I started I went out with only six plates, so I had to learn very quickly how not to waste a shot. I made it a habit to shoot sparingly, and I still do.

Do you crop your pictures?

Now, no. The picture of Solange was taken in 1929. The photograph was cropped because there were no long lenses then, and there was more of the picture than I required. I don't crop my pictures any more – I include the whole photograph. It's wonderful to include the entire thing.

Have modern smaller cameras made things easier for you and given you greater freedom?

It's the same. I'm still photographing the same kinds of image. You make fewer mistakes with exposure, but for me photography is about content – not the camera.

Opposite: *Solange,* Neuilly, 1929.

Renée à Biarritz. Piscine de la Chambre d'Amour, August, 1930.

Opposite: *John Kennedy*, Cap d'Antibes, 1953.

J.H. LARTIGUE

Sarah Moon

Sarah Moon lives and works in Paris. Although she spent much of her early life in England and went to an English public school, there is no doubt that she is utterly French. After a happy childhood she drifted into modelling at the age of nineteen. At this she was successful, working regularly for such magazines as *Elle* and *Marie Claire*. Also in this period she worked as a stylist, arranging props and clothes for photographic sessions.

With no clear-cut sense of direction, indeed almost by accident, she began taking intimate pictures of her fellow models during the long waiting periods in studios and dressing-rooms. Later she graduated to taking photographs for individual models' portfolios. In this way her work came to the attention of the progressive 1960s' fashion world. Soon, her talent acclaimed by the more forward-looking fashion editors such as Caroline Baker, Meriel McCooey and Molly Parkin, she was working regularly for innovative publications like *Nova* and the *Sunday Times Magazine*.

In 1968 she began her long association with the fashion house Maison Cacharel and her uniquely individual style – dreamy, sensuous, romantic, impressionistic – became widely recognized. In 1972 she photographed the prestigious Pirelli calendar and she has produced other calendars for Mitsubishi and Philips. Her work appears in magazines such as *Vogue* and *Harper's Bazaar* and she spends much time doing advertising photography.

Recently she has become involved in the making of television commercials for, amongst others, Cacharel. She is currently involved in a black-and-white feature film which she also scripted and for which she received a French government grant. Her photographic book, *Souvenirs Improbables*, is in the process of compilation.

Although both her outward appearance and her work suggest a shy and introverted personality, Sarah Moon has great tenacity and determination. Her immediately recognizable technique and composition, and her unique ability to capture mood and drama in a still photograph, assure her place among the most important and innovative fashion photographers of our time. Her work formed part of an exhibition of fashion photography at the Photographers' Gallery, London, in 1972 and another at the Rochester Gallery, Paris, in 1977. She took part in a show of women photographers at the 1974 Photokina exhibition in West Germany and has had solo exhibitions at the Delpire Gallery in Paris in 1975 and 1981.

Charlie Girl. The Pier,
commission for *Nova*,
Paris, 1960s.

How did you get into photography?

It all started with modelling, and even that was a coincidence. Someone asked me if I would pose for pictures and as I had nothing else to do at the time I agreed. I was nineteen and I was in the street when I met Susan Archer, a model-turned-photographer. She was the first to photograph me. At the time I was married to a painter and he thought modelling would be a good way of life for me, so I took it up. For myself I had no strong feelings about taking up a career in modelling. I knew nothing about that world.

Photography came later. At first I took photographs of models hanging round the studio waiting, or in the dressing-rooms. Then some of the girls needed photos for their portfolios. Fashion photography was very exciting in the late 1960s. I was already making a living as a model and so I could accept or refuse work, pick and choose. I started in England where everything was happening with magazines like *Nova*, and people like Molly Parkin were very creative. People would see my pictures and say, 'OK, I'll give you five pages. Do what you like.'

From the very early days you seemed to have a distinctive style.

You know I feel that that is my limitation, but at the same time I think that one can only have so many visions. I was so lucky to have the freedom to feel and to capture what I felt. It's not until you put one step in front of the other that you begin. You don't know what you want to do or achieve until you start to work and to experiment. So many photographers have had their originality crushed by working for people who dictated their style and gave them too little freedom to develop and discover their own path. I found my way but at first I was walking in the dark and I was lucky to be allowed to do so. Even now I like to hear people discussing my photographs as I find it sheds light on what I am trying to do. I make discoveries about my own work and motivation from such comments.

How do you set about taking a picture?

Today my technique is still to set the scene, to get the mood and the atmosphere right and then to wait and see what happens, hoping for the accident that will provide the correct moment to expose the film. To take an example – these pictures that I call 'Charlie Girl', which I did for *Nova*. For this shoot I did the casting in London. I just couldn't find the right child and so Caroline Baker, the Fashion Editor, and I went down to Brighton anyway with the model. All of a sudden, when I was walking down the beach, my luck changed and I saw these two children coming towards me with their dog. Quite naturally they evoked the image that I have captured. The shot of the girl and the boy on the pier was a lucky accident, not preconceived at all. I was wandering about above them and when I looked down I saw the girl and the child talking to each other beneath me. That was the picture.

Another example is this one of the girl walking her dog along the tree-lined avenue. I love this picture. It's my favourite. I was actually shooting another shot for a calendar at the time, but the model turned away at a break in the shooting and I shot this picture for myself.

Suzanne aux Tuileries,
Paris, 1974.

Two Girls with a 'Cat',
commission for English
Vogue, England, 1976.

Have you had any other happy accidents? They remind me of Ansel Adams' remark about fortune favouring the prepared mind. I think you mentioned that the cat picture was an example of this. Can you tell me about this photograph?

Yes. I am intrigued by masks and I had this idea about doing a picture of a man with a cat's face. What I wanted here was the feeling of two women relating to a sick cat. I don't quite know how the moment happened. I didn't tell the two models that the cat was supposed to be sick. If you put people into situations, eventually they will respond to the mood. It's just a question of waiting for the natural response. Actually the assignment was to show these two pullovers. This was an editorial rather than an advertising project and so it was enough merely to show the sweaters – I was not required to emphasize them. I love to do editorials because they are a good trampoline for one's imagination. You can see the product in this photograph, but it's not at all what the photograph is about.

Of course sometimes there is no 'accident', and on other occasions there are 'accidents' that I don't catch.

Do you find it difficult to analyze what is distinctive about your work?

Yes, it *is* difficult, but it is also valuable. As I talk to you I actually find out what I want to photograph. It clarifies things for me. As you know, I've recently been working on a book of my photographs and as a result have been giving them a lot of thought. This analysis of my pictures is unusual for me. I have seldom done it. Now I'm a little more conscious of what I do and try to do. I've found out, for example, that I like my images to be familiar to me, almost to have a feeling of *déjà vu* when I look through the lens. What I recognize and like to see is mood, the atmosphere of a scene that somehow tells a story.

In the cat picture there's a mood of tender concern for a gentle creature that does not feel well, a mood of sadness and pity. Unless I can recognize this quality in a picture, there's no picture there for me.

You mentioned that your distinctive style was also a limitation. Have you thought of extending your photographic range?

I have thought about it, but something I have come to realize is that I never photograph reality. That's a reason I could never do reportage. It's not my thing – not my way of working or my vision. I could never go out into the street and take a photograph. Also I would be incapable of photographing somebody without their agreement. I can't bear to be pushy, to intrude. People forget how cruel the camera can be – it seems often to reveal more than the naked eye. I've always been interested in fat people and old people, but I could not take advantage of them. So reportage would contravene my moral code, whereas fashion is perfect for me. It's not so much the clothes, but the beauty of the shapes and colours that appeals to me. But I also think there's a ceiling to fashion and it's a low one – you can bump your head against it. At the end of the day the real purpose of fashion photography is to serve the client and sell the product. Everything that you as the photographer add to it by way of story and mood is for yourself alone.

I know that you have become interested in making movies and your television advertising for Cacharel must take up a lot of your time. Is that the way you want to go?

Yes, I work a lot for Cacharel. It's a wonderful challenge to create a mood in thirty seconds or a minute. It's an exercise in condensation. I suppose in some ways I see my photographs as a single frame in a movie film. When you look at my photographs you can't escape the thought of what has gone before and of what will follow. They capture the moment and reveal a situation that has both echoes from the past and implications for the future.

So in this way making movies is a natural progression for me. Also it's new to me, and that's exciting. I've taken fashion pictures for ten years now and sometimes one repeats oneself.

Can we talk a bit about your technique?

I have a very simple technique. I don't work with flash. I use daylight and also use tungsten. When I don't know something I ask – either my assistant or another photographer. Luckily I have a lot of friends who are photographers. Things often go wrong. One should remember when looking at a collection of a photographer's work that one is only seeing the successful images.

The picture of the twins is an excellent example of your technique, and the lighting is very interesting. Can you explain how you achieved this effect?

I was commissioned to shoot this picture of twins in colour, but I did these shots in black-and-white for myself. I often do that.

My main technique is to use grain. I use as much as I can, although everybody tells me this is wrong and that I should make sharper images. Now in this picture the back light has strengthened the grain, and this has heightened the mood. But when using

Sarah Moon

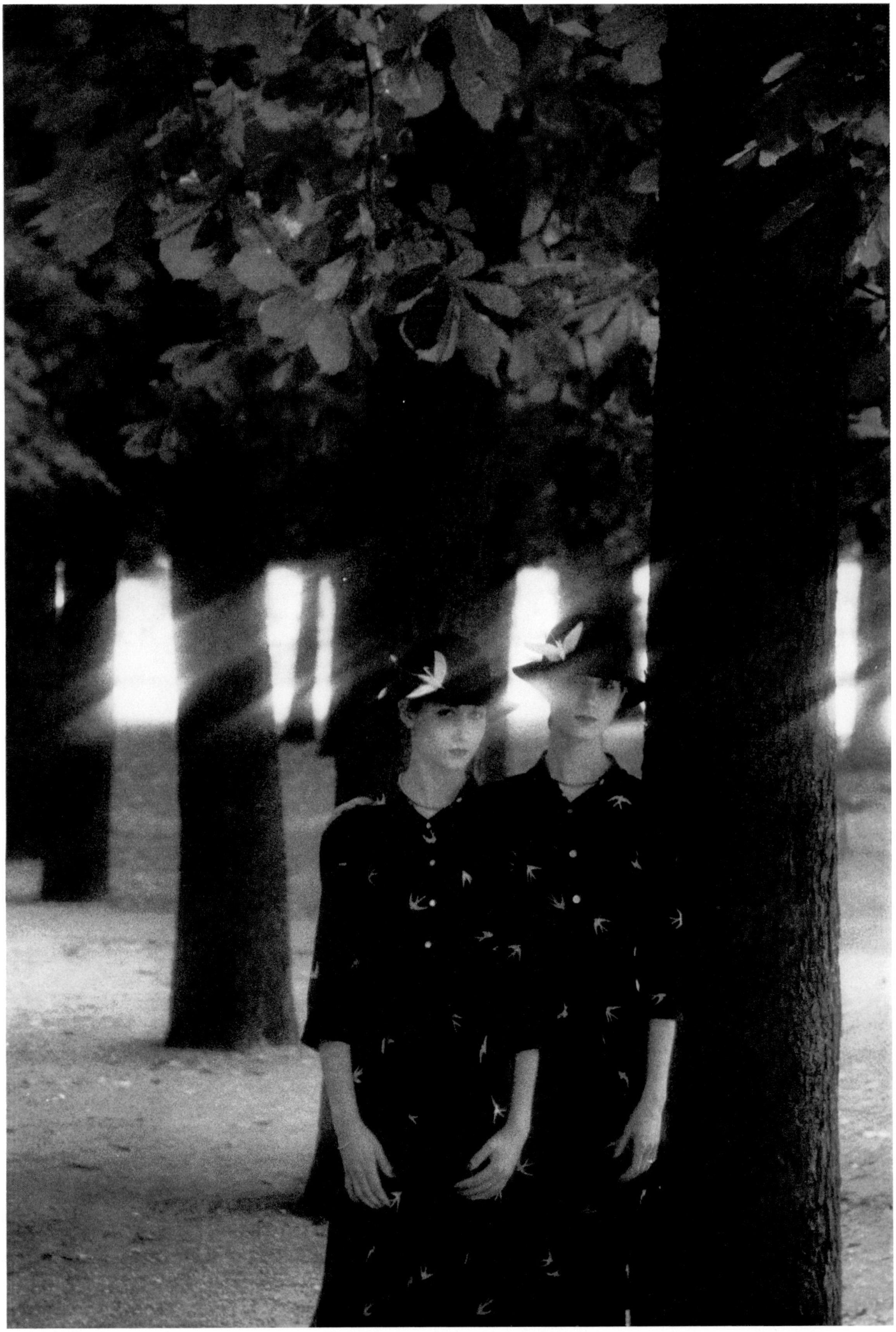

back light like this you must equilibrate by balancing the light with a sheet or a reflector positioned in front of the subject. If you don't equilibrate you end up with a silhouette. It's important to realize that what you see with your eye is not always what the camera sees. Through the lens it may not look like a silhouette, but without equilibration it will become one on the film.

Do you prefer black-and-white to colour?

Yes. I like to shoot in colour only when I can choose the colours. Black-and-white is more dramatic, further removed from reality.

What colour film do you use?

For many years I used GAFF. It was sheer agony when they went bankrupt. Now I use high-speed colour film and push it to get grain. Actually now that I'm used to it the effect is better, but I used GAFF for eight years. I like a lot of grain in my photographs and I don't like them to be too sharp, although recently my work has changed a bit and the pictures are becoming more clear.

You use lighting to heighten the graininess of your photographs. What else?

Soft-focus filters, different diffusers, sometimes voiles. I have no hard and fast technique. It depends on the mood that I want to portray. I can't say, 'I always do this, or that.' Tri-X pushed and recording film are good for grain.

Do you usually work with the same lens?

I never use short lenses. I work a lot with a zoom and never know exactly the length that I'm using, but it's usually 70mm, 80mm or even more. Sometimes I use a very long lens, but never wide-angle. One of the reasons I like a long lens is that it eliminates a lot of space. I have a problem with space – it's very difficult for me to deal with it. If I used a wide-angle I would have all that extra space in my pictures and that's just not my way of visualizing things. I suppose you could say that I see life a bit more cropped than other people! One of the advantages is that I never need to crop my pictures afterwards because I do it while I'm shooting. Of course I feel that the photograph should dictate the choice of the lens rather than the other way around, and it depends very much on the location and the shape of the room. I've used a 400mm for outside shots when I wanted a special effect, but usually it's around 100mm. I never go below 50mm.

What about cameras?

To me the simpler the better. I use 35mm only – never large cameras. I work with Nikon and Olympus. I especially like a Nikon because it's built like a tank and I can rely on it. I always use a tripod.

Although you live in Paris you use an English printer. Why?

I've never done my own printing and Bill Rawlinson is great. He works alone and cares about his work, never rushing things. It would take me some eight or nine hours to produce just one print of the quality that he makes, and even then it wouldn't be as good as his.

How long does an assignment usually take you?

If I'm lucky, perhaps half a day. I'm a slow and methodical worker and often it takes a whole morning just to get the models ready. I plan in advance, and I've usually found

Twins, commission for Cacharel, Paris, 1980.

Sarah Moon

the location days before. Then I start to gather together a team I know – hairdresser, make-up artist and stylist. I explain to them all exactly what I'm going to do. The day of the shoot is organized like a military campaign. Then it's just a question of waiting for the right moment. All I say to my models is 'Just wait.' I hear myself saying it over and over again. In my photography one is always waiting – for the light, for the models, for the right moment. I get incredibly anxious and I go on shooting until I'm tired and everybody else is tired. The more you work, the more chance you give yourself to succeed.

Do you ever dream up an idea and then take it to a magazine or company and try to 'sell' it to them?

Yes. I do it a lot. This photograph of the dress is an example of that. For some unknown reason I had always wanted to do photographs of dresses on hangers, so I went to *Vogue* and suggested the idea. I borrowed an apartment that I liked, one that had lots of mirrors, and shot the dress through a plain, modern looking-glass. That was how I got the eerie, shimmering, almost ghost-like effect.

Dress Seen through a Mirror, commission for French *Vogue*, Paris, 1977.

It seems that composition is important in your photographs. The picture of the three girls is a good example.

For me there is first the lighting, then the composition and finally the expression. Yes, I like the composition in this photograph. I wanted to do something very decadent. I had seen this child before and been struck by the fact that she had the face of an old lady. There is something so dramatic in her face.

Three Girls, commission for Italian *Harper's Bazaar*, Paris, 1978.

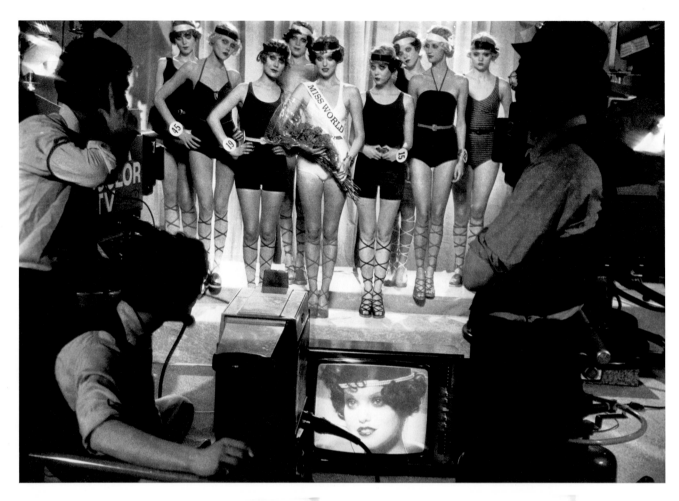

Beauty Contest,
commission for the
Sunday Times, London,
1975.

Your Pirelli calendar was much admired. How did that come about?

They approached me and said, 'We would like you to do the calendar. You can do anything you like as long as it's women, and you can go to the Bahamas.' I told them that I don't work in sunlight and I don't photograph girls getting out of the water in wet shirts, so I didn't need to go to the Bahamas. I told them that what I wanted was to find a house, fill it with women and create moods of intimacy. So that was another example of me being allowed to do what I wanted. It was the same with the picture of the beauty contest. I shot this in 1975 for the *Sunday Times*. I was told that I could do what I liked as long as the bathing costumes were well shown. I used a video studio as the setting. It's very unusual for me to work in a studio and of course I could not use daylight, so I had no back light to diffuse the picture.

Which photographers have influenced you most?

Very few fashion photographers. Guy Bourdan is incredible. He can create something out of nothing and leave his own unique stamp on it.

If you had to sum it up, what would you say that photography has meant to you?

I think that it's perhaps the only way to learn how to see. It is an intensely individual vision and I think that every child should learn how to take pictures. Ten different people taking a shot of the same flower will produce ten unique images. By repetition the image gradually becomes more precise and you slowly build up your own style. In the end it may even be confusing to know about the artist's conception of his own picture, about his motivation, because the viewer must project his own imagination on to the photograph and see what he *wants* to see. That may be his best way of getting in touch with the artist's mind, because often the artist himself is not conscious of what he is doing. Words are a poor substitute for the actual photograph, which must speak for itself. You can talk about your approach, but not about the art itself.

Are you able to evaluate your own pictures – comparing one with another?

I find it difficult to grade my pictures in terms of quality, to say what is good and bad, and I have a terrible problem in choosing photographs for a book or exhibition. Possibly this is because once a photograph has arrived I feel that I no longer identify with it properly because it has already led me off on a path to something else. I have progressed away from it.

Arnold Newman

Arnold Newman was born in New York City in 1918, when America's boom years were running out of steam, a fact which cast the shadow of poverty over much of his early life. His parents, victims of the 1929 crash, ran hotels in Miami and Atlantic City. From 1936 to 1938 he received a working scholarship from the University of Miami to study art, but in 1938 financial difficulties forced him to take a job in a chain of portrait studios.

He moved to Philadelphia and became friends with a group of students who were working under Alexei Brodovitch, art editor of *Harper's Bazaar*, at the Philadelphia School of Industrial Arts. Taking portraits during the day, Newman experimented at night in the dark-room. Although he was influenced by the work of Walker Evans and by other photographers of the Farm Security Administration, he also experimented with photographic abstractions. He was, as he himself well admits, obsessed with photography.

In late 1939, tiring of the constant moves demanded by his job, he accepted an offer to manage a coupon studio in West Palm Beach, Florida – people would exchange a small sum in a local store for a coupon which entitled them to have their picture taken by Newman. He bought a 5×4 press camera and devoted all his spare time to photography.

In 1941 he was at a crossroads in his career, uncertain whether or not he had a future in photography. He travelled to New York to seek the advice of Beaumont Newhall who, with Alfred Stieglitz and Dr Robert Leslie, encouraged him to continue. Leslie offered him a joint exhibition with his childhood friend Ben Rose. The show, at the A–D Gallery, was attended by Ansel Adams and a Newman photograph was bought for the permanent collection at MOMA. His career as a professional photographer was launched.

The success of another exhibition, *Artists Look Like This*, in 1945 established his unique style, which has been called 'environmental portraiture'. Newman made use of the sitter's natural environment to amplify and expand his personality and to pinpoint and comment on his particular contribution to the world.

Newman decided to give up what had become a lucrative business in Florida and in 1946 he moved to New York City. In that first year he was commissioned by *Life* to

'We don't take pictures with cameras – we take them with our hearts and minds.'

171

photograph Eugene O'Neill and by *Harper's Bazaar* to do the famous portrait of Igor Stravinsky, which at the time was rejected by Brodovitch.

From his early days Newman has been interested in abstractions and has a keen eye for shape, geometry and composition. With his sophisticated lighting technique and formidable mastery of the scientific side of photography, skills that he prefers not to emphasize, Newman brings his brilliantly creative mind's eye to bear on the subjects of his portraits, explaining them and exposing their relationship to the world that they have influenced.

Today Newman, father of two sons, lives in New York City with his wife. His one-man exhibitions have included *Artists Look Like This*, at the Philadelphia Museum of Art, in 1945–6; shows at the Art Institute, Chicago, 1953; at the Fourth Biennale Internazionale della Fotografia, Venice, in 1963; and at the International Museum of Photography, Rochester, New York, in 1972; and *The Great British*, at the National Portrait Gallery, London, in 1979.

———•———

How did you start in photography?

Initially I wanted to be a painter. When I graduated from high school in 1936 I wanted very much to study at the Art Students' League, which was *the* school in the 1930s. I hadn't enough money to go north. I got a scholarship to the University of Miami, which in those days had only two art teachers. They were members of an old establishment family and they were absolutely the right teachers for me at the time. At that time, too, some friends introduced me to the work of Picasso, Matisse and others.

It was a working scholarship and I had to do things like painting scenery and organizing classes in addition to my studies. I was working eight hours a day, seven days a week. Commuting the fifteen miles from home took a lot of time and at night I was totally exhausted. That was the way things were in the 1930s.

I didn't think of myself as being deprived. In fact I think that if there is a single common thread in the early lives of artists it is this tremendous urge to work.

But, paradoxically, didn't that very shortage of money turn you in the direction of photography rather than fine art?

Yes. I just couldn't continue financially and I was offered a job by Leon Perskie, a friend of the family, who had studios in department stores in several different cities. Until then the main focus of my life had been art, but immediately I took that job and moved to Philadelphia I fell under the spell of photography.

Some friends of mine, including Ben Rose and Sol Mednick, were studying in Philadelphia at the School of Industrial Arts, now the College of Fine Arts, under Alexei Brodovitch. He was art director of *Harper's Bazaar* and had a tremendous influence on photography. During the day I would take 49-cent portraits for a wage of $16 a week. Even *then* I was underpaid! At night we'd stay up and take pictures. So all at once I fell in love with photography and forgot about art. I never went back to painting. That was the end of it.

Did your family encourage your photographic ambitions?

Yes. It was most out of character for a nice, middle-class Jewish family, struggling to put food on the table, actually to arrange art lessons. In those days it was insanity, but that's what they did. Sadly, my father died a week before my first show. We came from Atlantic City and the local newspaper carried the announcement of his death on the same page as an article about my exhibition. The fact that I was actually encouraged by my parents to study art was the most unusual feature of my childhood.

Do you believe that artistic talent is innate?

I'm convinced of it. Any great artist will eventually admit that you can't teach art. You can open doors and windows and if somebody has talent you can encourage them. Or you can crush them – I've seen that happen, too. You can't create an artist out of nothing, although you can help with everything from technique to showing them what has gone before and making a favourable emotional and creative environment for them. Real artists, however, will work and survive despite bad atmospheres and difficulties, because they have the drive and the power.

Do you belong to any particular 'movement' in photography?

There are many different ways to 'feel' and many different paths. Therefore to say that this group or this one person and his followers are the only ones is nonsense. I take pictures the way I do because I'm the kind of person that I am. I don't say that I do it better than anybody else. It's simply different, because I'm a different person from everybody else. My way is not necessarily the only way or the best way – it is *my* way. There were a lot of people who copied me when they started, but then we all start by copying somebody else. Eventually, hopefully, people break loose into their own individual direction or style . . . into their own adaptation. Not everyone will be another Weston or another Sheeler. People must become themselves. That's what's so terribly important.

Were you influenced more by painters than by photographers?

No, not really. Although I was forced into photography in a way, I was well aware of the Farm Security Administration and the work of Steichen. He, Stieglitz, Man Ray – they were all great influences on me – Walker Evans too. They were brilliant, honest photographers. Man in particular was a very good friend. Of course I had always been excited by painters – the Flemish masters, Rembrandt, Michelangelo, Picasso, Braque, Matisse. I was influenced by all these men and out of it I developed my own style. We must all build on what has gone before. If we were influenced by nothing it would be pointless – some absolute genius might invent the wheel all over again!

What camera did you use in the early days?

I borrowed a camera from an uncle of mine, a $3\frac{1}{4} \times 2\frac{1}{4}$ Contessa, and put a viewfinder on it. From the first 12-film pack came the first picture in my book *One Mind's Eye* – the woman nursing the baby. I had begun to realize right from the beginning that a photograph wasn't a painting – that it required a different kind of conceptual approach. I knew and understood that automatically.

Did you ever foresee the emergence of photography as a major art form such as it has become today?

We all had a very strong feeling about it. I think we knew it would happen, but we didn't know when. Stieglitz was the one who had this concept of showing photographs. It has been much maligned. People have suggested that it is very precious, but they have misunderstood the whole point. They fail to understand that if an individual image has something to say it makes absolutely no difference whether it is a painting, a drawing, a photograph or a print. It goes on the wall to give enjoyment and to reiterate, continuously, a statement.

Of course some pictures lose one's interest and become boring. It may be because a news item is no longer topical, a model no longer trendy, or a certain way of shooting a picture no longer in vogue. Photojournalism can suffer from this. Then you get rid of it or tuck it away. But the really great artists don't have this problem.

What do you feel about purely commercial photographers? Can they be 'honest' photographers?

They, too, can be great artists. Horst, for example, was a marvellous fashion photographer, doing purely commercial work. He was photographing beautiful women in beautiful dresses. About two or three years ago my wife and I went to see a show of his. I was stunned. The concept of his photography was so strong – the creative content so powerful – that it over-rode whatever the immediate requirement for the picture was. When you looked at those pictures you no longer saw just beautiful photographs – they were photographs which had mystery. You see this is a form of fantasy, and there is nothing wrong with fantasy provided that it is presented as such.

There is one particular portrait artist who presents fantasy as fact. He wants you to believe that everybody he photographs is the most important person in the world at that moment, that his eye is on the horizon and he's leaving the whole world behind him. It's nonsense, because it's inbelievable, but on the other hand he wants you to believe what he is saying. That's impossible. So he's presenting fantasy as fact and you have to discount it.

Horst, and very many others – Beaton, for example – who did this sort of thing were marvellous and produced beautiful pictures. In the same way Steichen's portraits, which were terribly theatrical and full of fantasy, were wonderful because they were presented as such. To see these things is comparable to enjoying the mystery of a Rembrandt. In our century the Ashcan School, the group of eight who showed extreme poverty, are about as far from Rembrandt and fashion pictures as it's possible to be. However the essential thing that links them is that these works are all honest. You accept them for what they are. You must believe in the photographs you do. If you don't believe in your photographs you can't continue, particularly if you're not making a living out of it!

You mentioned your friendship with Man Ray. The piece in your dining-room reminds me of his work.

You mean the cut-out violin shapes? Well, yes and no. I would say that it's closer to Cubism, but then again it isn't Cubism. Actually – this is what's so funny – cut-outs like that were really not shown till later. This was just something I went off and did on my own. There were rumours in the 1940s about Picasso's cut-out shapes, but this was done in the early 1940s before I had heard these rumours.

Do you know of any other interesting instances of people producing the same idea, though in complete isolation from each other?

I think many people arrived at the same conclusions at the same time – Fox Talbot and Daguerre and others, for instance, were all working on the fixing of the image of the camera obscura around the same period. It's a matter of who comes first. I used to know a great scientist who said, 'It's not necessary to be better than anybody else, it's just necessary to be one day earlier.' He was talking about science, but it seems to me that the better painters, artists, photographers and sculptors are always one day earlier than the ones who are not so good. The imitators are often slick and may even be more polished, but they lack the power of the originators.

I started doing portraits in the very early days. For the first two or three years I would go from one studio to another working for two different bosses. Otherwise I was experimenting, a student trying out different ideas, to see how they related to me. Farm Security Administration, Cubism, various forms of Abstractionism – I tried all those as well. But from the moment I started to do portraits I was excited by them. Even so, after being in photography for two and a half years I wasn't sure whether or not I should continue. At the time I was working in an isolated manner in West Palm Beach running this cheap coupon studio. So in the spring of 1941 I came to New York to visit Beaumont Newhall, who was then the one and only creative museum curator of any stature anywhere in the world. I wanted his advice about my future in photography. When I showed him my work he got so excited he sent me over to see Stieglitz, two blocks away. I was also told to see a Dr Robert Leslie, an unbelievable man who still runs around the world although he's in his nineties. It was he who encouraged me to continue and therefore changed my life. He offered myself and Ben Rose, my childhood friend, a two-man show.

What sort of work did you show then?

It was pure abstraction and Farm Security Administration. The piece we discussed earlier was in the show. I hadn't done any *experimental* portraiture at all. In this period I had begun more and more to think about applying these visual concepts to portraiture, and so I figured I'd come to New York to see who had been doing it and to try to work.

And did you?

For a while I was able to work, but my principal client was unemployment compensation! I was living from hand to mouth, sleeping on the couch of a cousin of mine. I had $10 that my father was able to spare, an old, borrowed overcoat and one suit of clothes. I used to take my clothes to the cleaners and have them pressed while I waited in the back. It was a tough time, but an exciting one. I was meeting everyone from Mondrian to Léger. I would visit Stieglitz frequently at his request and from there I would walk over to Mondrian. To me it was the most exciting period of my life. I was making these portraits and bringing them in for criticism to Beaumont Newhall, and he was buying them for the Museum of Modern Art. I was all of twenty-three and I had been taken up by the art world. I would get a $25 job here or a $15 job there – I was able to squeeze by. Things were tough financially but not creatively. I was beginning to experiment with portraiture. It was a time of explosive development and I have never looked back. It was difficult to buy the right equipment. Luckily, though, we don't take pictures with cameras – we take them with our hearts and minds.

I enjoyed your book Artists *very much. How did that come about?*

I had a big show at the Philadelphia Museum called *Artists Look Like This*. I did not actually photograph the artists as a series, although I made a book out of it. I used the artists as a group of people who, collectively, were the most interesting visually out of all the portraits I was doing at the time. I did it in order to experiment with ideas about portraiture. The subjects were obviously interesting and it was a wonderful opportunity for me to meet my idols. They sort of picked me up and then handed me on from one to the other.

That show ran from December 1945 into 1946. *Life* gave me two and a half big pages and the *New York Times Magazine* two pages. Then the war was over and everybody was saying, 'Do you want to work for us?' Actually I had been going a long time by then. You know how you always read that an actor is an overnight success, when in fact he has been struggling on for years? Well, I had exhibited at MOMA at Christmas 1941. The show was called *Ten Photographers*. We each exhibited one photograph and they were for sale at $10 each. Not one of them sold. It was important to have faith in those days!

Can we talk about some of these photographs here?

My first assignment was for *Life* magazine, to do a portrait of Eugene O'Neill, and shortly after that I was asked to do the Stravinsky portrait by *Harper's Bazaar*. So you could say that I started at the top. I think this is a very successful photograph. I was at my very best that day. Nothing could go wrong. I have a lot of excellent photographs from that session. It's funny because it was a very difficult situation – in one way artificial. Everybody thinks it was Stravinsky's piano, but it wasn't – it was borrowed. It wasn't even shot in his home. He was staying in a New York hotel room and I was asked to photograph him in a couple of days. All I could think of was this big, beautiful piano shape that I had always admired – strong, harsh, linear, like Stravinsky's work in a sense. I knew exactly how I was going to light it and the composition was already in my mind. The whole thing came together and it really worked.

I am credited with having invented 'environmental portraiture', but actually I've never used the term. I do like to photograph people in their homes, studios and offices, but what is important is that the environment should be symbolic of the subject. That was the case with the Stravinsky portrait. I got to know Stravinsky quite well. He was a far more conventional man than Picasso, whom I also photographed. Stravinsky had a lovely home in the Hollywood Hills and a 'legitimate' family, quite unlike Picasso, and yet the two men were close friends.

Harper's rejected this photograph, by the way, although they were rather pleased to print it a bit later on!

Igor Stravinsky, New York, 1946.

Your portrait of Claes Oldenburg is a striking example of an original approach to portraiture.

When I made the print of the Claes Oldenburg portrait I found it rather boring. Suddenly I realized that the sense of fun, of the unusual and unexpected, that characterized Oldenburg's own work could be applied to my print. So I thought I would experiment and tear the print down the middle so that the tear almost touched him on the head. It worked. The only other thing I can tell you is to repeat what Imogen Cunningham said years ago, 'If you don't like it that's your problem, not mine, because I love it.'

Claes Oldenburg, New York, 1967–72.

Sir Ralph Richardson and Sir John Gielgud, London, 1979.

This double portrait of John Gielgud and Ralph Richardson is particularly fine. How did it come about?

The Gielgud and Richardson portrait was shot for *The Great British*. I had a wonderful time shooting this picture. There was a good deal of joking and badinage, and it is one of my personal favourites. It was conceived, of course, in the usual desperation. I wanted to do it in a theatre, or somewhere that might reflect the theatre, but that was impractical because of other photographs that I had already taken in the series. So I shot it in an alley-way alongside the theatre where Sir Ralph was appearing in a play, and Gielgud kindly agreed to come along. I like the abstract black-and-white quality of the paint on the wall, and the texture and weathering of the bricks.

The idea of the photograph was to capture the somewhat Pinteresque relationship that existed between the two men. I had seen *The Homecoming* and *No Man's Land* and the way that they acted together, and I think I was successful in this photograph in getting something of the flavour of it – the way they are together and aware of each other and yet, at the same time, apart. You can't always translate such a concept on to film, but I think in this instance it was extremely successful.

This picture of Marilyn Monroe does look very spontaneous.

It's a rarity. I was shooting candid pictures and actually this is just a small portion of a 35mm shot, which has been pushed like mad. The texture isn't artificial. It was shot with Tri-X film rated at 1200. It was after dinner and there was almost no light in the room. I thought it was completely typical of her so I made a big blow-up of that head. It's been a very popular photograph.

Arnold Newman

Marilyn Monroe, Beverly Hills, 1962.

Surely the Krupp portrait was not so spontaneous?

Krupp had agreed to pose for me, but when I arrived in Essen and presented myself at the Krupp works I was told by an executive that the session had been cancelled. I knew that I had to act quickly if I was to get the photograph, and I thought fast. Then I slammed my fist down on the table and said, 'How dare you do this to me! I have come all the way from the United States.' It was no way to talk to neo-Nazis and they were clearly shocked that I had taken this outrageous line with them. They thought that a photographer was somebody to be ordered around, and here I was demanding to see Krupp. The executive went away and when he came back he was awestruck as he told me that Krupp would see me after all.

I isolated myself with Krupp on this platform, which I had asked them to build, and I used the available lighting, altering it just enough to make him look sinister. As far as I was concerned the whole day worked beautifully. The executives insisted on taking me out to dinner. While we were eating somebody went through my camera case and copied the Polaroid that I had made of the shot. Subsequently I was told that I was *persona non grata* in Germany. But they had no legal power to stop me using my pictures.

So I did what I had wanted to do and showed this evil man who had chained munitions workers to the machinery when there were bombs dropping so that they couldn't run for cover – people who only a few years before had been ordinary citizens, doctors and lawyers and had been turned into slave labour. That was why I took the attitude that I did. I felt justified, metaphorically speaking, in putting a knife in his back.

And your Piet Mondrian portrait . . . ?

I think the Mondrian picture explains itself. He was a rather stiff man, but at the same time warm. In fact his personality rather resembled his work and it certainly reflected his living quarters, which, at one time or another, he deliberately made into works of art. So my picture is not an imitation of Mondrian – it is an interpretation of Mondrian and his work.

Did you consciously imitate Francis Bacon's work in your portrait of him?

Now when I took this photograph of Bacon in his studio he just happened to be standing beneath the skylight, with this bulb hanging down. I realized to my astonishment that it resembled some of his own paintings. It was pure accident. I said, 'For God's sake don't move', pulled the camera over, got into position and clicked the shutter. Strangely enough one New York critic said it was a contrived photograph, but in fact it was one of the most spontaneous pictures that I have ever taken.

Can you talk a little about your technique and equipment?

There's not much to say. I adapt to my surroundings. Nothing else matters. After all, the camera is nothing more than a box with a pin-hole at one end and a piece of film at the other.

I don't make notes on what exposures I have used in the past. Carefully delineated shapes are important to me in my work and therefore I try to use the longest possible exposures – up to several seconds sometimes, which can be a bit long even with a tripod to someone who is used to moving around. Other times it may be a second.

I check out the various lenses when new ones come on the market, but I don't keep buying the latest equipment. That doesn't produce better photographs. I like to emphasize to students that great masterpieces have been taken with primitive equipment.

Alfred Krupp, Essen, Germany, 1963.

Overleaf left: *Piet Mondrian*, New York, 1942.

Overleaf right: *Francis Bacon*, London, 1976.

181

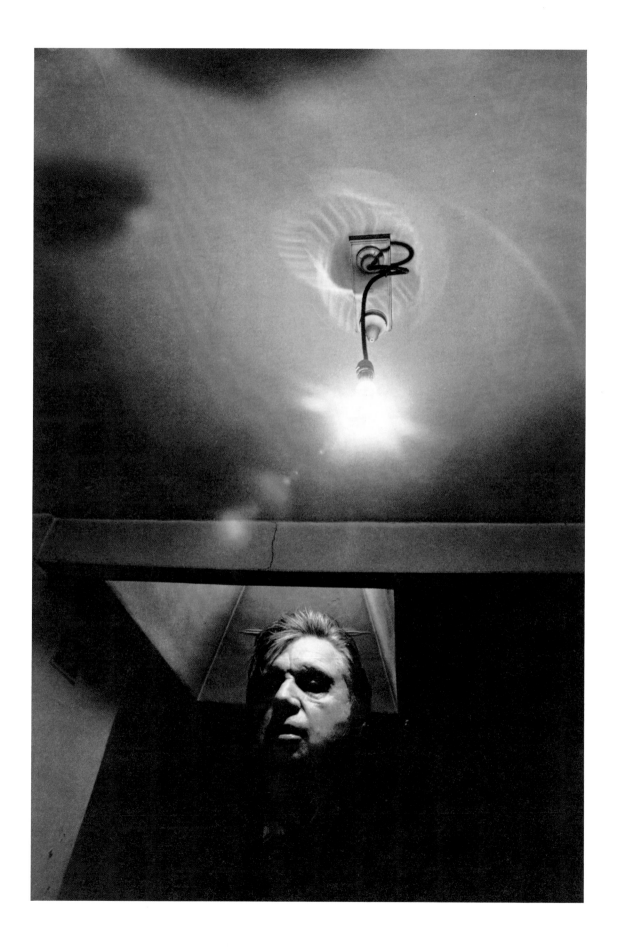

Equipment is merely a tool and should be used as such, but you must know it and feel comfortable with it.

When I have the choice I like to work with black-and-white rather than with colour because I have greater control. Occasionally I use colour and get good results. And I like to use the fastest film that is available for the camera that I am using.

Most of the pictures we have discussed have been shot on 5×4 format. In recent years I have begun to use 35mm and 120 because now you can get the quality, and those cameras give you greater mobility. The difference to me between a 5×4 and 35mm is the difference between a big oil painting and a watercolour. There are some subjects that just don't lend themselves to big oils and vice versa. One is not better than the other – they are simply different. Some subjects lend themselves to both. The 35mm is good for images that move about, have poor light and insufficient depth of field and so on. It's good for colour, too.

What about lighting?

I prefer to use natural light, and when this is impossible I add flash using a 'bounce' technique, reflecting it against a light wall or a piece of cardboard – something like that. It looks more natural doing it that way and also round, soft, reflected light delineates objects a lot better than direct light. Once again I must stress that I'm not saying that direct light is bad, just different. You can use direct light to create shadows that are as strong as the object itself, but you must know that that is the effect you are after. I use it sometimes if I think the subject requires it, but mostly I use 'bounced' light. Still you must never have fixed rules, otherwise you won't get anywhere. Actually I think my lighting techniques are fairly obvious and they are not really that important. It is the use of the subjects, the way they are positioned, perhaps in a purely abstract way or applying the technique of abstraction, that is important.

Can you sum up your philosophy?

Yes. Photography is not about cameras, film paper and enlargers. The most important thing that I possess is my ideas – the way that I see things and the way that I interpret that seeing process.

Helmut Newton

Helmut Newton, the high priest of erotic photography, was born in 1920 in the decadent society of post-First World War Berlin. He was brought up in Germany, but is now an Australian citizen. In 1936 he began his photographic career as an apprentice to the German photographer Yva, who specialized in fashion photography, nudes and portraits of dancers. For the last twenty years Newton has lived in Paris with his wife June, who is herself an accomplished photographer working under the name Alice Springs.

From 1960 to 1970 Newton worked regularly for French, Italian, English and American *Vogue* as well as for *Elle, Marie Claire, Jardin des Modes, Nova, Queen* and American *Playboy*. During the last few years he has worked more or less exclusively for French and American *Vogue* and for the German magazine *Stern*.

In 1979 he was the subject of a British documentary made for Thames Television by Michael White. He has had one-man exhibitions at the Photographers' Gallery, London, in 1976; the Nicholas Wilder Gallery, Los Angeles, in 1976; the Marlborough Gallery, New York, in 1978; the American Center, Paris, in 1979; and the G. Ray Hawkins Gallery, Los Angeles, in 1980.

For me, decadence is phoney and unnatural, and I like the unnatural.'

———— • ————

Your work often depicts women in subservient positions, and has a flavour of cruelty and violence. Yet you seem to be able to transform the stock-in-trade of the porn shop into something glamorous – how do you achieve that?

I once took some pictures for *Vogue Hommes*, featuring Hermès products, and *Life* magazine chose one of them as an illustration of the decadence of the 1970s. I am in favour of my work being described as decadent. For me decadence is phoney and unnatural, and I like the unnatural. I don't consider whips, spurs and saddles as being violent in any way. They are certainly erotic devices, and they go back for hundreds of years.

Hermès is quite extraordinary. They have one glass case containing spurs, and another with the most beautiful whips made of the finest leather, and yet another case exhibiting the most expensive saddle you could imagine. It's all very chic and sophisticated – really Hermès is the ultimate sex shop.

187

Though your photographs are highly erotic, they are always in 'good taste'. How do you avoid crossing the borderline into pornography?

I don't believe in good taste. It's very boring. I do have a built-in safety valve that stops me shooting pornography, even when I have the opportunity to do a really dirty picture. Perhaps that's one of my failings. For example in this photograph, *Californian Fingernails*, I had the opportunity to go further, but I didn't. The model would have been quite willing to do anything at all.

Incidentally, this photograph is a good example of the importance of geography in my work. I couldn't possibly have shot it anywhere else in the world but Los Angeles. I would never have thought of shooting a picture like this in Paris. I arrived in Los Angeles last December and wanted to do something that was the epitome of the town. One thing that everybody notices about the place is the length of the women's fingernails. It's not just the rich and idle with these long talons – the shop assistants have them too. They're built out of porcelain – quite horrible. Well, I'd been thinking about this idea for two months and when I found this girl I had her fingernails built up even longer than she would normally wear them. It cost me $1000. The way she would use them was quite fascinating, for instance as a coke spoon – I have pictures of her extracting the coke out of a little vial. I know nothing about drugs and I'm not interested, but it was amazing to see that.

Actually the girl was a trans-sexual, but I didn't know that when I asked her to pose for me. I saw her in a restaurant and she had such a beautiful face and wonderful legs that I fell for her immediately. Usually I work only with professional models, but on this occasion my wife made me approach her. After we had done the pictures the model asked me why I hadn't bothered to check out her body before the shoot. She said, 'After all, I could have been a guy.' It was a good question, because usually I will never photograph anyone before I have seen them in the nude. It was the first time in my life that I had done a session without seeing the girl with no clothes on – she was just so fantastic looking.

By the way, I shot the picture on a 35mm SLR using Tri-X. For lighting I used a 350 watt lamp with a reflector.

Can you expand a bit about the relevance of geography to your work?

Well, I love the big cities – Paris, New York and Los Angeles. I especially love Tinsel Town. I love its superficiality. I prefer Astroturf to real grass, for instance. The concept of the American 'girl next door' is incredibly sexy, but then I also love the 'rich bitch' type that goes to the Polo Lounge at the Beverly Hills Hotel. Paris is a wonderful city for me because I know it so well and I understand a certain class of French woman, and can therefore portray her very accurately. It is important to me to have the detail in my photographs absolutely accurate, and so it helps to know both the town and the people who live there. For example, if I did a shot of a French businessman undressing a girl in a car it would be a Citroën DS – the car of a middle-class bureaucrat – and the paper on the seat beside her would be *Le Monde*, the establishment newspaper. I would never take such a photograph using a Rolls or a Cadillac. It would have to be essentially Parisian.

Now England has always been a problem for me. I have never been able to take a good photograph there. I spent the unhappiest year of my life in London in the 1950s when I was under contract to English *Vogue*. I was there the other day, walking in Green Park. Nothing was happening that in any way inspired me, whereas I can walk for five minutes through a Paris park and there is so much going on I can get hundreds of ideas.

Also I don't understand English women. The only ones I have ever found interesting are Glenda Jackson and Charlotte Rampling.

Helmut Newton

When you go walking in the park, do you take a camera?

No, I used to, but not any more. It's better to remember the visual experience and to keep it filed away and cross-referenced in your head. I like my photographs to be meticulously prepared in advance. The actual photography is very fast but the organization is a long, long process. Sometimes the idea for a picture may take several years to germinate.

That suggests you are not keen on producing reportage photographs. Is that so?

I worked on three occasions for the *New York Times*. Once it was a great success, but the other times it was just terrible – like working for a church magazine. I won't be doing that again.

In the past, although you have been taking pictures of nudes they have merged into fashion photographs. Do you agree?

Yes, absolutely, but in my recent work I've been trying to get away from that. These nudes have been compared to sculpture – nothing really to do with photography. I've been doing them for a year and a half and they represent a complete change in my work.

I had been intending to do a book with the painter Allen Jones, but the project didn't come off mainly because I couldn't see what my contribution would be. He does it so much better. Now this photograph is pure Allen Jones. I very much like the fact that

Californian Fingernails,
Los Angeles, *c.* 1981.

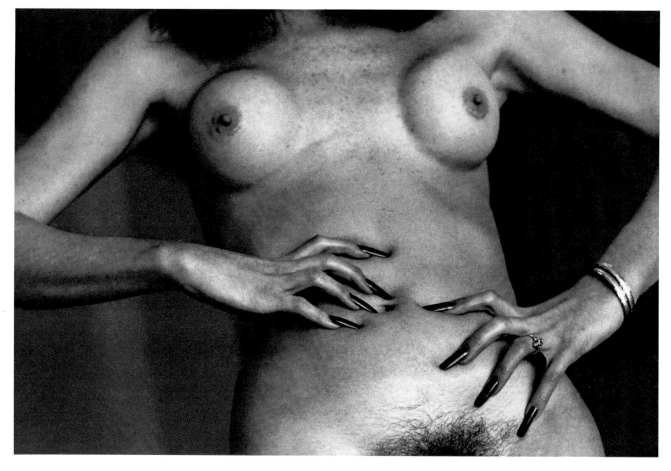

there are no accessories except for the high-heeled shoes. They are there for aesthetic reasons. I like the way they make the muscles at the back of a girl's legs protrude and the shape that they give to her body. Bare feet and tennis shoes give a woman a completely different stance. I always notice in the South of France that when a model comes on to the beach in bathing suit and tennis shoes nobody looks at her twice. With high heels everyone would turn their heads – no question.

The photograph was shot on Tri-X, using a Reflex 6×6. I shone an indirect 500 watt flood at the ceiling and for the light on her legs I turned a 35mm slide projector upside down and directed it at the girl.

You spoke there of the influence of Allen Jones. In this photograph of the 'wrapped torso' do I detect Christo's influence?

This photograph was taken when I was in the South of France on commission for German *Vogue*. It is very interesting that you remark on the influence of Christo, although I didn't consciously think about it when taking the photograph. At the time I was after a sado-masochistic image, but with the girl being very strong. I am a great admirer of Christo – in fact I have recently bought my wife several of his works.

This shot was taken on 2¼ square format using Tri-X film. I shot it in natural sunlight at mid-day. I like the hard shadows you get by doing that.

Untitled, South of France, *c.* 1980.

Opposite: Untitled, Paris, *c.* 1981.

191

And what about women's fantasies?

Of course women do have their own intensely erotic fantasies, and often it is centred on the dominance of the male. I know women who talk about men as total sex objects. One particular friend, a very 'proper' lady, told me quite freely that her fantasy was to be raped under a bridge by a truck driver. My wife, for example, had a great attraction to the man who delivered the wood. He was very surly and extremely dirty. June was mad about him. As we got to know him better he lost his sulkiness and became quite friendly. Also he cleaned himself up a bit. Now June has lost all interest in him because he's become too nice!

So I think my pictures are erotic but they are not cruel and they are not demeaning to women, because I think that many women share the fantasies that these photographs depict.

What is your reaction to your pictures?

Of course, for myself my pictures are not erotic, although I hope they are for other people. All the work and organization that goes into them means that they lose their power to excite me. If, for example, I took a quick snap of someone for whom I felt something, that recaptured a memory or a dream, that could be erotically interesting for me – but because of the way in which my pictures evolve they have no power to excite me.

What relationship do you have with your models?

A very unemotional one. I just direct them to my requirements. I don't test them. If I like them I give them the job immediately, although, as I mentioned just now, I have to see their bodies first – either physically, or in a clear photograph. My relationship with models is very automatic, very impersonal.

Who influences you at the moment?

I get a lot of ideas from people who write on photography. Also I get very stimulated by literature – people like Roland Barthès and Schnitzler. I found many passages in a book by Barthès extremely illuminating. Some of these ideas I have written down and will be trying soon on Los Angeles. However it's one thing to have them down on paper and quite another to have them on film. More and more now, when I get an assignment for a magazine, I ask to be allowed to work with a writer. It's so much better if in addition to seeing the photograph you can read about the ideas behind it. The writer sees things that influence me and my pictures illuminate his writing. There is a certain pretentiousness about showing a photograph on its own.

Can you talk about this photograph of Roselyne? It seems you like to photograph powerful women.

This photograph was part of a series taken in a château in the west of France. It was a dark and rather gloomy house with a weird atmosphere. We had to do the shots at times when the other house guests were not around. Luckily the servants were very discreet about it.

Some people say that the girls I like are too big and certainly I've always been interested in tall girls. Personally I like a big back. I love that overblown look. In the early days I used to photograph fashion models with the shape of skeletons, but as one gets older one's ideas become more definite, developed, pure. What I love to do is to photograph a nude doing exactly what she would be doing in an elegant dress.

Opposite: Untitled, France, 1975.

Do you have any difficulty selecting what you feel are your best photographs from contact sheets?

I have missed so many good pictures from contact sheets in the past that now I let them sit around the studio for as long as possible so that I lessen the chance of missing anything.

Do you use a lot of equipment?

No. My equipment is tremendously simple. I am not remotely interested in the hardware of photography. In terms of lighting I have hardly ever used Balcars – perhaps only ten times in my life. I prefer to use available light and when it's not strong enough I amplify it with a photoflood. Usually one is enough, even when there are a lot of people in the photograph. I use anything from 250 watts to 500, but usually 500. Sometimes I mix in light from a blue globe tube – that's electric light supposedly balanced for daylight: it cools the pictures down a bit. I am always changing my technique and experimenting with it.

Some years ago, in the 1960s, I brought back the fashion of the 'ring' light. Originally this consisted of a heavy metal and wooden ring filled with photofloods through which the photographer would shoot. Later, of course, with the invention of strobe, medical photographers used the ring flash concept to take some wonderful photographs. I tried out my ring flash then on one of the Rome collections. When I got the transparencies back I was shocked to find all those red eyeballs. I immediately thought that I'd better throw the ring away as I'd no idea how it had happened. Then I thought it looked quite funny and so I published the photographs anyway, and of course all of a sudden everybody just loved pictures of girls with red eyeballs. Later I found out how to avoid it, but it took me a while. You only get red eyes with a ring flash in a dark studio, not when you mix in daylight with it. The reason for this is that in a studio dimly lit by a single 'model' light the girl's pupils dilate and the retina is exposed. The red colour is the result of light bouncing off a large, exposed retina. The answer is to have other lights on the girl, two or three stops less than the ring flash of course, and in that way the retina is 'guarded' by more constricted pupils. It was fun for a bit but it was just a gimmick.

My basic lighting is the 500 with the blue light mix. You mustn't add in too much blue light or it will incline towards magenta. For black-and-white on location I use cardboard to shade with – to manufacture shadows. Either I do it or my assistant does. It's all done with imagination and no expense at all. I think the clients are always rather disappointed that they don't get more in the way of equipment – just a 500 watt globe and a bit of old cardboard.

That's very interesting about your lighting, but what about cameras and lenses?

The one thing I consider really important is that the lenses are in good condition. I test them religiously to make sure they are sharp.

I prefer to use a $2\frac{1}{4}$ square format camera. My recent exhibition was shot on two old Rolleiflex cameras that I have had for ages. Usually when I'm not using a camera any more I sell it or give it away. I hate cluttered cupboards. People tell me that I ought to use a 10×8 camera to overcome grain, which I hate, and to get the right texture to a woman's skin, which is important to me. But I reckon that if you can't get the image on a $2\frac{1}{4}$ square you can't get it at all. Who wants to go lugging a thing around that shows the picture upside down? I'd have to have the woman standing on her head to see her the right way up!

I use the standard 80mm lens and also the very high-quality 135mm that they made years ago. With 35mm I use 35, 40 or 50mm lenses. I use telephoto only for special effects or when I can't get near enough to the subject. I don't mind 35mm used vertically but I hate the long, narrow, landscape format, which I find unpleasant. I love the square format – typical of the 1930s which was the era of the Rolleiflex, and also the period when I had my photographic education. I just love the 'feel' of it, and it simplifies composition of the picture. With the 35mm there is not enough room on the negative – you can't cram enough information on the side of the picture. I always find the things going on around me so interesting that I like to get a little further away from the subject than is strictly necessary in case anything unexpected happens on the periphery. You can always cut it off later if it doesn't work. With the 35mm, if you don't have it right you don't get the picture. There's nothing to cut off.

Do you use a wide angle on 35mm to give yourself more room?

No – never. The quality suffers if you have to blow up an already small central image, having cropped off the edges. I like definition and I don't like grain. I'm not the world's greatest technician, but I am aware of the very best my lab. is capable of giving me and that's what I want – definition and room on the negative. I don't even mind there only being twelve shots. I like being forced to stop.

The Rolleiflex factory has gone out of business. What's your opinion of the Hasselblad?

I have always disliked it. The design is bad. I hate the way the image disappears when you click the shutter on a slow exposure. It's archaic. With the Rollei, a twin-lens reflex, the image is there all the time. For me they were the greatest camera builders in the business.

What about film?

For black-and-white, Tri-X. For colour-reversal film, Ektachrome. I used to be a Koda-chrome fiend, but now I've given it up as I'm looking for a more funky colour. Koda-chrome is incredibly versatile. It has to be – amateur cameramen use it in their Insta-matics and they get incredible results, taking pictures against the light and in conditions when I wouldn't even dream of attempting a shot. They are very wise to use Koda-chrome. It has become a 'serious' film, and you can't get the same brightness with Ektachrome. However there's something about Ektachrome that's almost unprofessional and I like that.

Do you use Polaroids?

Yes. They're very useful. It's vital to use one for checking lighting before a shoot, especially when it's complicated. Also on trips it's a good method of keeping track of what you're doing when you know you won't see the finished article for a while. When I come back from a trip the first thing my wife says is, 'Can I see the Polaroids?' Occasionally when she eventually sees the contacts she might say, 'They're not as exciting as the Polaroids.' Then sometimes it becomes a bit of a hang-up and I wonder if maybe I should be shooting everything on Polaroids, although that would be a little complicated. With Polaroids you get a sort of spontaneous, relaxed quality that my pictures often lack. But there's not much I can do about it. I just have to have all the details absolutely right. I go mad if a hair is out of place.

Do you shoot much film on a session?

Very little. I have done jobs where I've only shot one roll.

It seems to me that you impose a strict discipline on your photographs — whose subject matter, incidentally, often alludes to themes of discipline. Do you yourself prefer to work on commission with clear guidelines laid down for you to follow?

You're quite right. I find it terribly hard when I'm the boss. I know much better what the magazine wants or what the client wants than what I want. I haven't got a clue what I want. It could be anything at all.

So you don't often take experimental shots?

No. I always need a whip behind me. I'm very bad at getting off my arse unless I've been commissioned. Also the ideas that excite me are often expensive to put into practice. I have a way of working to beat the system. I take my ideas to *Vogue* or *Vogue Hommes* and shoot it as 'editorial'. Then I shoot my own personal pictures on the same session. That way everyone is happy.

Are you happy to restrict yourself to the small number of magazines you work for now?

When I was younger I worked for a lot of magazines — now I concentrate on just a few. I think one's pictures have a certain style that becomes associated with specific magazines. Pictures that work well in French *Vogue* might look totally out of place in *Elle* or *Marie Claire*. Also I think the magazines like to get together a team of photographers who are all working, if not on the same wavelength, then at least at the same level.

Apart from anything else I don't have enough ideas to work for lots of magazines — you see, magazines are the starting point for me in the developing of an idea. I am very lucky to have such a good relationship with French *Vogue*. No other magazine in the world would give me so much space and have such confidence in me.

Bibliography

Ansel Adams

Taos Pueblo, San Francisco, 1930; Boston, New York Graphic Society, 1977.

Making a Photograph, London, New York, The Studio, 1935, 1938, 1948.

Sierra Nevada: The John Muir Trail, Berkeley, Archetype Press, 1938.

Illustrated Guide to Yosemite Valley, San Francisco, H.S. Crocker Co., 1940; San Francisco, Sierra Club, 1963.

A Pageant of Photography, San Francisco, San Francisco Bay Exposition Co., 1940.

Michael and Anne in the Yosemite Valley, New York and London, Studio Publications, 1941.

Born Free and Equal, New York, US Camera, 1944.

Basic Photo Series, Boston, New York Graphic Society, 1948–50, reprinted 1976: 1. *Camera and Lens*; 2. *The Negative*; 3. *The Print*; 4. *Natural Light Photography*; 5. *Artificial Light Photography*.

My Camera in Yosemite Valley, Boston, Houghton Mifflin, 1949.

My Camera in the National Parks, Boston, Houghton Mifflin, 1950.

Death Valley, Boston, New York Graphic Society, 1963; San Francisco, 5 Associates, 1954.

Mission San Xavier del Bac, San Francisco, 5 Associates, 1954.

The Pageant of History in Northern California, San Francisco, American Trust Co., 1954.

The Islands of Hawaii, Honolulu, Bishop National Bank, 1958.

Yosemite Valley, San Francisco, 5 Associates, 1959.

Death Valley and the Creek Called Furnace, Los Angeles, Ward Ritchie Press, 1962; Redwood City, 5 Associates, 1970.

Introduction to Hawaii, Redwood City, 5 Associates, 1964.

Fiat Lux: The University of California, New York, McGraw Hill, 1967.

The Tetons and the Yellowstone, Redwood City, 5 Associates, 1970.

Ansel Adams, New York, Morgan and Morgan, 1972.

Singular Images: A Collection of Polaroid Land Photographs, Hastings-on-Hudson, New York, Morgan and Morgan, 1974.

Ansel Adams: Images 1923–1974, Boston, New York Graphic Society, 1974.

Photographs of the Southwest, Boston, New York Graphic Society, 1976.

The Portfolios of Ansel Adams, Boston, New York Graphic Society, 1977.

Polaroid Land Photography, Boston, New York Graphic Society, 1978.

Yosemite and the Range of Light, Boston, New York Graphic Society, 1979.

The New Ansel Adams Photography Series, Boston, New York Graphic Society: 1. *The Camera*, 1980; 2. *The Negative*, 1981.

Eve Arnold

Unretouched Women, London, Cape, 1977; New York, Knopf, 1976.

In China, London, Hutchinson, 1980; New York, Knopf, 1980.

Flashback, New York, Knopf, 1980.

David Bailey

David Bailey's Box of Pin-Ups, London, Weidenfeld & Nicolson, 1964.

Goodbye Baby and Amen, London, Condé Nast, 1969.

Beady Minces, London, Matthews, Miller, Dunbar. 1973.

Warhol by Bailey, London, Matthews, Miller, Dunbar. 1974.

Another Image – Papua, New Guinea, London, Matthews, Miller, Dunbar, 1975

Mixed Moments, London, Olympus Optical, 1976.

Trouble and Strife, London, Thames & Hudson, 1980; New York, Rizzoli International, 1980 as *Mrs David Bailey*.

David Bailey's Book of Photography, London, Dent, 1981.

Bailey's NW1, London, Dent, 1982.

Bill Brandt

The English at Home, London, Batsford, 1936; New York, Scribner, 1936.

A Night in London, London, Country Life, 1938.

Camera in London, London, New York, Focal Press, 1948.

Literary Britain, London, Cassell, 1951.

Perspective of Nudes, London, New York, Bodley Head, 1961.

Shadow of Light, London, Bodley Head, 1966; New York, Viking Press, 1966. Republished London, Gordon Fraser, 1977; New York, Da Capo, 1977.

The Land, New York, Da Capo, 1976; London, Gordon Fraser, 1975.

Bill Brandt: Nudes (1945–1980), London, Gordon Fraser, 1980; Boston, New York Graphic Society, 1980.

Bill Brandt: Portraits, London: Gordon Fraser, Knoxville, University of Texas Press, 1982.

Harry Callahan

The Multiple Image: Photographs by Harry Callahan, Illinois, Institute of Design Press, 1961.

Harry Callahan, Fotographia-Galeria, 1963.

Photographs: Harry Callahan, Van Riper and Thomoson Inc., 1964.

1967: Photographs by Harry Callahan, Hallmark Cards, 1966.

Harry Callahan, New York, Museum of Modern Art, 1967

Callahan, Aperture, 1976; London, Gordon Fraser, 1977.

Water's Edge, Lyme, Conn., Callaway Editions, 1980.

Harry Callahan: Color, Tucson, Matrix Publications, 1980.

Robert Doisneau

La Banlieue de Paris, Paris, 1949.

Sortilèges de Paris, Paris, 1952.

Les Parisiens ou tels qu'ils sont, Paris, Robert Delpire, 1954.

Instantanées de Paris, Paris, Arthaud, 1955; New York, Simon & Schuster, 1956 as *Paris*.

1,2,3,4,5, Lausanne, Editions Claire Fontaine, 1955; New York, Lippincott, 1956.

Paris Parade, London, Thames & Hudson, 1956.

Pour que Paris sort, Paris, Cercle d'Art, 1956.

Grosses de Paris, Paris, Jeheber, 1957.

Marius le forestier, Paris, 1964.

Le Royaume d'Argot, Paris, 1965.

Epouvantables épouvantails, Paris, Hors Mesure, 1965.

Catherine la danseuse, Paris, 1966.

Témoins de la vie quotidienne, Paris, 1971.

My Paris, New York, Macmillan, 1972.

Le Paris de Robert Doisneau et Max-Pol Fouchet, Paris, Editeur Français Réunis, 1974.

Manuel de St Germain des Prés, Paris, 1974.

The Boy and the Dove, New York, Workman Publishing Co., 1978; Paris, 1979 as *L'Enfant et la Cólombe*.

La Loire, Paris, Editions Filipacchi, 1978.

Trois secondes d'éternité, Paris, 1978; Boston, New York Graphic Society, 1979 as *Three Seconds to Eternity*.

Le Mal de Paris, Paris, 1980.

Elliott Erwitt

Photographs and Anti-Photographs, Greenwich, Conn., New York Graphic Society, 1972; London, Thames & Hudson, 1972.

Observations on American Architecture, New York, Viking Press, 1972; London, Thames & Hudson, 1972.

The Private Experience, London, Thames & Hudson, 1974; New York, Crowell, 1974.

Son of Bitch, New York, Grossman, 1974; London, Thames & Hudson, 1975.
Recent Developments, New York, Simon & Schuster, 1978.

Ralph Gibson
The Strip, Los Angeles, Robert Kennedy, 1966.
The Hawk, Indianapolis, 1968.
The Sonnambulist, New York, Lustrum Press, 1970.
Déjà-Vu, New York, Lustrum Press, 1973.
Days at Sea, New York, Lustrum Press, 1975.
Contact: Theory, New York, Lustrum Press, 1982.
Mit Konkreten Bildern die Welt Ordnen, Hamburg, 1980.

Horst
Photographs of a Decade, New York, J.J. Augustin, 1944.
Orientals, New York, 1945.
Patterns from Nature, New York, J.J. Augustin, 1946.
Vogue's Book of Houses, Gardens, People, 1968, New York, Viking Press, 1968.
Salute to the Thirties, New York, Viking Press, 1971; London, Bodley Head, 1971.

Yousuf Karsh
Faces of Destiny, New York, Prentice-Hall, 1946; London, Harrap, 1947.
Portraits of Greatness, Toronto, University of Toronto Press; New York, London, Thomas Nelson and Sons, 1959.
In Search of Greatness, Toronto, University of Toronto Press, 1962; New York, Alfred P. Knopf Inc., 1962; London, Cassell, 1963.
The Warren Court, New York, Macmillan, 1965.
Karsh Portfolio, Toronto, University of Toronto Press, 1967; New York, London, Thomas Nelson and Sons, 1967.
Faces of Our Time, Toronto, London, University of Toronto Press, 1971.
Karsh Portraits, Toronto, London, University of Toronto Press, 1976; New York, Little, Brown, 1976.
Karsh Canadians, Toronto, London, University of Toronto Press, 1978.

André Kertész
Enfants, Paris, Editions d'Histoire et d'Art, 1933.
Paris vu par André Kertész, Paris, Editions d'Histoire et d'Art, 1934.
Nos Amis des bêtes, Paris, Editions d'Histoire et d'Art, 1936.
Les Cathédrales du vin, Paris, Etablissements Sainrapt et Brice, 1938.
Day of Paris, New York, J.J. Augustin, 1945.
André Kertész, Photographer, New York, 1964–5.
On Reading, New York, Grossman Publishers, 1971.
Foto, Budapest, 1972.
André Kertész, Sixty Years of Photography, New York, Grossman Publishers, 1972; London, 1972.
J'Aime Paris: Photographs since the 1920s, New York, Grossman Publishers, 1974.
Washington Square, New York, Grossman Publishers, 1975.
Of New York, New York, Knopf, 1976.
Distortions, New York, Knopf, 1976.

André Kertész, New York, Aperture, 1977; London, Gordon Fraser, 1977.
From My Window, Boston, New York Graphic Society, 1981.

J.-H. Lartigue
The Photographs of Jacques-Henri Lartigue, New York, Museum of Modern Art, 1963.
Les Photographies de Jacques-Henri Lartigue: un album famille de la belle époque, Lausanne, 1966; New York, Guichard–Time Life Books, 1966, as *Boyhood Photographs of Jacques-Henri Lartigue: The Family Album of a Gilded Age*.
Diary of a Century, New York, Viking Press, 1970; London, Weidenfeld & Nicolson, 1970; Paris, 1973 as *Instants de Ma Vie*.
Portfolio of J.-H. Lartigue, New York, Witkin-Berkey, 1972.
Women, New York, Dutton, 1974; London, Studio Vista, 1974 as *Femmes*.
J.-H. Lartigue et les autos, Paris, Editions du Chêne, 1974.
Mémoires sans mémoire, Paris, Editions du Chêne, 1975.
Lartigue 8 × 80, Paris, Delpire Editeur, 1975.
Jacques-Henri Lartigue, London, Gordon Fraser, 1976; New York, Aperture Books, 1976.
$8\frac{1}{2} \times 8\frac{1}{2}$, London, Gordon Fraser, 1977.
Les Femmes aux cigarettes, New York, Viking Press, 1980.
Mon Livre de photographie, Paris, 1977; New York, Barron (forthcoming) as *My Photography Book*.
Les Autochromes de J.-H. Lartigue, 1912–1927, Paris, 1980; New York, Viking Press, 1981; Ash and Grant, 1981 as *The Autochromes*.

Sarah Moon
Modinsolite, Paris, 1975.

Arnold Newman
Happytown Tales, Coral Gables, Florida, Parker Art Printing Association, 1944.
Bravo Stravinsky, Cleveland, Ohio, World, 1967.
One Mind's Eye: The Portraits and Other Photographs of Arnold Newman, Boston, New York Graphic Society, 1979; London, Secker & Warburg, 1974.
Faces USA, New York, London, Amphoto, 1978.
The Great British, Boston, New York Graphic Society, 1979; London, Weidenfeld & Nicolson, 1979.
Artists: Portraits from Four Decades, Boston, New York Graphic Society, 1980; London, Weidenfeld & Nicolson, 1981.

Helmut Newton
White Women, New York, Stonehill Publishing; London, Quartet Books, 1976; Paris, Editions Filipacchi, 1976.
Sleepless Nights, New York, Congreve; London, Quartet Books, 1978; Paris, Editions Filipacchi, 1978.
Special Collection: 24 Photo Lithos, New York, Congreve, 1979; London, Quarto, 1980; Paris, Editions Filipacchi, 1979.
Helmut Newton, Paris, Editions du Regard, 1981.
47 Nudes, London, Thames & Hudson, 1982.

Index

Page numbers in *italic*
refer to the illustrations